ENCHANTED GARDEN

An Innovative Culinary Experience:

CONNECT...CREATE...COOK

by
Jodi Felice

OZARK MOUNTAIN PUBLISHING

PO Box 754
Huntsville, AR 72740
www.ozarkmt.com
479-738-2348 or 800-935-0045

For permission, or serialization, condensation, adaptions, or for catalog of other publications, write to: Ozark Mountain Publishing, Inc., PO Box 754, Huntsville, AR 72740, Attn: Permissions Department.
This publication contains images from CorelDRAW®9 which are protected by the copyright laws of the U.S., Canada and elsewhere. Used under license.

Library of Congress Cataloging-in-Publication Data
Felice, Jodi - 1960 -
"The Enchanted Garden" by Jodi Felice
A cookbook based on magical herbalism to inspire emotional and spiritual growth through cooking. Promotes awareness of the positive energy all plants and herbs possess.
1. Cooking   2. Herbalism
I. Felice, Jodi, 1960 -   II. Title
Library of Congress Catalog Number: 2007925467
ISBN: 978-1-886940-75-8

Cover Art and Layout by www.enki3d.com
Book Design: Julia Degan
Book Set in: Times New Roman, Lucida Handwriting, Unicorn
Published by

PO Box 754
Huntsville, AR 72740

www.ozarkmt.com
Printed in Korea

CONTENTS

INTRODUCTION

I grew up in an Italian family where preparing a meal meant more than just satisfying your hunger. In my home, food, family and friends went hand in hand. The moment you took your first bite, you knew that you where loved. The sharing of a meal, even til this day, always evokes a warm sense of home. I am not a professional chef nor do I have any formal training in the culinary field. For me, cooking simply means having the freedom to express my spirit.

Sometimes, all we need is one word, smell or taste to awaken a positive feeling. My passion for cooking led me to discover the magical and powerful energies that herbs, spices, vegetables and fruits possess. My desire to share these experiences inspired the creation of 57 original and interactive gifts.

The concept is based on ancient magical philosophies. Herbs, spices, vegetables and fruits have long been known to possess the powers within them to manifest needed change. These exotic, aromatic and magical energies stimulate our emotions, motivate our minds, aid our physical bodies and nurture our spirit. Using both this knowledge and my own intuitive senses, I was able to connect with the individual plant and receive its specific intention. The task of each recipe that follows will be to inspire you to connect with these powerful energies and allow them to enhance your ability to create positive change.

I grew up with all of the recipes that are included and still enjoy them today. They have all been passed down and around between family and friends. Like many cooks, I don't measure the ingredients before putting them into a recipe. I do my best to approximate the quantities in each. If there are flavors that you don't like, then omit them. Don't be afraid to adjust any of the recipes to meet your own taste. I don't like complicated recipes, so each one is simple and easy to follow.

All of the recipes are full of magical energy, so it's important to pay attention not only to the main plant, but to all the minor energies that go into creating these recipes. Once you have become familiar with all the magical intentions, this process will become much easier. The most important thing is to have fun and enjoy the experience.

1

ACKNOWLEDGMENTS

There are many people in my life who have inspired, believed and supported me through the creation and completion of this book. I am grateful for this opportunity to express my gratitude and say thank you to some of the most important people in my life.

MOM: Thank you can never fully express how grateful I am to have you as my mother. My passion for cooking came from you. You taught me that the food always tastes better when it's made with love. You always inspire me with your courage. Thank you for always making my favorite crumb cake every time I come to visit. But most of all thank you for not saying "GET A REAL JOB" even when I know you really wanted to.

I've been blessed this life time to have two fathers.
    To my father in Heaven: Thank you for teaching me to be patient. Although you did not get a chance to see any of my work, I always feel you smiling down upon me.
    To my father MIKE: You are always there for me and that is the true definition of a father. Even though you didn't understand the concept at first, you believed enough in me to help get this business started. Hands down, you make the best sauce in town. I'm grateful you're in my life.

MICHELLE: You are an amazing woman, wife and mother. I love that you share the same passion for cooking. I laugh at how excited you get just talking about trying new recipes. Thank you for always being on my side. I'm proud and grateful that you are my sister.

PAT: My favorite brother-in-law. Thank you. I know you always have my back.

AMANDA and PATRICK: Thank you for being the inspiration for the kid friendly recipes and mommy for giving them to me.

MELISSA: My teacher, mentor and good friend. Thank you for Tuesday nights and for sharing all your wisdom, experiences and insight with us. I am very grateful to you for going out of your way to help me get this book published. You've helped me grow in every area of my life. I'm blessed to have you as my friend.

MAY: You have been here since the beginning of this venture. From faux finishes to hurricanes. Thank you for all positive insight and for always being there for me. I am grateful that you are one of my dearest friends.

LYNN MARIE: You are one of my most true and treasured friends. There is no way I would have gotten through the last couple of years without your constant encouragement and guidance. Thank you for always being there when I needed you. I'm grateful and blessed to have you as my friend.

DONNA Z: We go back a long way. Thank you for being excited for me when I started this business. Your encouragement and enthusiasm helped me believe in myself. You are my no muss, no fuss friend. I can always count on you to set me straight.

BRIDGET: We have known each other since we were 11 years old. I'm proud to say that you are one of my oldest and dearest friends. Thank you for never judging me and for always believing in my dreams.

To my SOPHIE GIRL aka "fat girl". Thank you for always licking up the crumbs off the floor.

OZARK MOUNTAIN PUBLISHING: Thank you to everyone. You've made my dream come true.

EMPOWERING YOUR PLANT

Empowering your plant aligns the vibrations of the plant with your intentions. This process increases the effectiveness of the magic.

To activate the magical intention, you must infuse your energy with the plant. Before using your magical plant, take a moment and hold it in your hands. Visualize your desired result and send it into the plant. When you're ready, add the enchanted plant into the recipe.

HERBS

Chamomile
Thyme
Basil
Parsley
Oregano
Garlic
Mint
Cilantro
Sage
Dill
Bay
Rosemary

My name is CHAMOMILE...
I hold the magical energy of
TRANQUILITY, INTEGRATION, MOTIVATION
and NEW BEGINNINGS...
I have a light, sweet apple-like taste.
My gift to you is FREEDOM...
Imagine that my energy surrounds you
and TRUST that you are SAFE and that
you are LOVED.

HERBS

CHAMOMILE TEA
Serves 4

2 1/2 cups boiling water
1 tbsp dried CHAMOMILE flower heads
Sugar or honey (optional)

Put chamomile into a cup, add boiling water, and let infuse for about 5 minutes. Strain and add sugar or honey to taste.

BEFORE YOU BEGIN, REMEMBER TO EMPOWER YOUR HERB (see page 4)

CHAMOMILE TEA BLENDS
Serves 1

2 tsp CHAMOMILE
1/8 tsp spearmint or peppermint extract
1/8 tsp finely chopped rosemary
or
2 tsp CHAMOMILE
1/4 tsp finely crushed star anise
1/8 tsp cinnamon
1/8 tsp vanilla extract

Mix ingredients together until well blended. Add to 1 cup of boiling water and let infuse for a few minutes or to desired strength. Strain and serve.

My name is THYME...
I hold the magical energy of
ANTICIPATION, PEACE, RENEWAL and
INSPIRATION...
I have a strong aroma and a
wonderfully woody flavor.
My gift to you is PATIENCE...
Imagine that my energy surrounds you and
TRUST that you are SAFE and that
you are LOVED.

HERBS

POTATO AND ZUCCHINI WITH FRESH THYME
Serves 4

2 medium zucchini	5 tbsp butter
2 large baking potatoes	1 large onion
1 tbsp chopped fresh THYME	2 cloves garlic, chopped
salt and pepper to taste.	

Trim the zucchini and potatoes and cut into 1 inch slices. Drop into a large saucepan of boiling salted water and cook for about 8 minutes. Drain well, dry the pan, and add the butter, onion, garlic and thyme. Saute for about 2 minutes or until the onion is tender. Add the potatoes and zucchini and season to taste. Stir gently to mix, cover, and cook over very low heat until the vegetables are tender.

BEFORE YOU BEGIN, REMEMBER TO EMPOWER YOUR HERB (see page 4)

CHICKEN CUTLETS WITH FRESH THYME
serves 4

oil for frying (any type you prefer)
1 large egg
4 boneless chicken breasts
2 cups flavored bread crumbs
1 tbsp finely chopped fresh THYME
3 good sized garlic cloves, chopped
1 tsp crushed red pepper (optional)
salt and pepper to taste

In a large frying pan, heat up approximately 1/4 inch oil (use more if necessary). In a small bowl, beat the egg with either a splash of milk or water. Mix together the bread crumbs, thyme, garlic, red pepper, salt and pepper. Pour onto a flat plate. Dip each breast into egg and coat with bread crumb mixture. Place chicken into hot oil and cook until golden brown on both sides.

My name is BASIL...
I hold the magical energy of KINDNESS,
POWER, DETERMINATION and PURPOSE...
My name means "king" and I am one of the
most important of the culinary herbs. My
sweet scent is strong and my taste delicious.
My gift to you is COURAGE...
Imagine that my energy surrounds you
and TRUST that you are SAFE and that
you are LOVED.

HERBS

TOMATO AND MOZZARELLA SALAD
serves 4

8 oz mozzarella, cubed
1 medium cucumber, cubed
1 medium red onion, thinly sliced
4-5 plum tomatoes, seeded & chopped
4 oz fresh BASIL, chopped
1/4 cup olive oil
2 splashes of balsamic vinegar
1/2 tbsp garlic powder
Salt and pepper to taste
1 loaf Italian or French bread

In a large bowl, add the cheese, onion, cucumber, tomatoes and basil. Then add the oil, vinegar, garlic, salt and pepper, and mix well. To let the flavors marinate, cover and refrigerate for about 30 minutes or serve immediately with the bread.

BEFORE YOU BEGIN, REMEMBER TO EMPOWER YOUR HERB (see page 4)

PESTO AND TOMATO TOAST APPETIZERS
makes about 20

1 cup BASIL leaves
3 cloves garlic
1/2 cup pecans
1/4 cup olive oil

1 loaf Italian or French bread
10 large sun dried tomatoes, cut
into thin strips
5 oz Parmesan cheese, shaved

To make pesto, mix the basil, pecans, oil and garlic in a food processor until the mixture is smooth. Toast the bread slices until golden brown on both sides. Spread the pesto evenly over the pieces of toast. Top each one with sun dried tomatoes and Parmesan cheese.

11

My name is PARSLEY...
I hold the magical energy of PROSPERITY,
ADVENTURE, CREATIVITY and JOY...
I supply a rich source of vitamins and
minerals. A sprinkle of my bright green
leaves provides color and a refreshing
flavor to a variety of dishes.
MY gift to you is ABUNDANCE...
Imagine that my energy surrounds you
and TRUST that you are SAFE and that
you are LOVED.

HERBS

STUFFED ARTICHOKES
Serves 4

4 large artichokes
2 cups flavored bread crumbs
5 cloves garlic, finely chopped
1 cup finely chopped PARSLEY
1/4 cup Parmesan cheese
1/4 cup & 2 tbsp olive oil
Salt and pepper to taste

Cut the top off of each artichoke leaving it flat; wash and spread open each leaf. Mix together the bread crumbs, cheese, garlic, parsley, salt, pepper and 1/4 cup oil. Stuff each leaf of the artichokes with the mixture and place in a large sauce pan of salted water. Make sure the water comes up almost to the top of the artichokes. Moisten the top of each artichoke with the remaining olive oil, cover, and cook over medium to low heat until the artichokes are tender.

BEFORE YOU BEGIN, REMEMBER TO EMPOWER YOUR HERB (see page 4)

ZUCCHINI, PARSLEY FRITTATA
Serves 4

3 cloves garlic, chopped
6 tbsp chopped PARSLEY
1 medium zucchini, chopped
12 large eggs
1 large tomato, seeded & chopped
4 oz heavy cream or milk

1 tbsp butter
2 tbsp olive oil
1 med onion, chopped
Salt and pepper to taste
PARSLEY for garnish

Heat the butter and oil in a large skillet and saute the onion and garlic until tender. Add the zucchini, tomato, parsley, salt and pepper. Cook over low heat until tender. Beat eggs and cream together; season to taste. Pour into skillet and stir to mix. Cook on low heat until eggs set. Place the pan under the broiler to brown the top. Slide out of pan and garnish.

My name is OREGANO...
I hold the magical energy of HARMONY,
COMPASSION, APPRECIATION and
GENEROSITY...
I am known as the "joy of the mountains".
I have a spicy aroma and a robust taste.
My gift to you is TENDERNESS...
Imagine that my energy surrounds you
and TRUST that you are SAFE and that
you are LOVED.

HERBS

CHICKEN OREGANO
Serves 4

4 chicken breasts on the bone, skinned
1 large onion, sliced
4 cloves garlic, chopped
2 heaping tbsp OREGANO
2 tbsp extra virgin olive oil
Salt and pepper to taste

Preheat oven to 400. Place chicken breasts in a pan. To keep it lean, remove the skin. Sprinkle the sliced onions all around and coat the chicken and onions with the olive oil. Season with garlic, oregano, salt and pepper. Add about 1/4 inch water on the bottom of the pan (this will create a nice gravy) and bake for 1 1/2 hours.

BEFORE YOU BEGIN, REMEMBER TO EMPOWER YOUR HERB (see page 4)

SALMON STEAKS & OREGANO SALSA
Serves 4

1 tbsp butter
4 salmon steaks 8oz ea.
1/2 cup white wine
2 tbsp OREGANO, chopped
1 tbsp tomato puree
1 small hot pepper (optional)

4 spring onions, chopped
8oz tomatoes, peeled
2 tbsp extra virgin olive oil
1/2 tsp sugar
Salt and pepper to taste
OREGANO to garnish

Preheat oven to 300. Butter a pan and put in the salmon. Add the wine, salt and pepper. Cover with tin foil and bake for 15 minutes. Let cool. Put the oregano, onions, hot pepper, tomatoes and all the remaining ingredients in a food processor and process in bursts until chopped (but not a smooth puree). Serve the salmon cold with the salsa and garnish.

My name is GARLIC...
I hold the magical energy of POTENTIAL,
INTEGRITY, ORIGINALITY and SUBSTANCE...
I have a very powerful flavor. I will lower
your pressure and purify your blood.
My gift to you is RELEASE...
Imagine that my energy surrounds you
and TRUST that you are SAFE and that
you are LOVED.

HERBS

SPAGHETTI WITH GARLIC AND OIL
Serves 4

12 oz spaghetti	8 tbsp extra virgin olive oil
5 cloves GARLIC, chopped	2 tsp crushed red pepper
2 tbsp of fresh basil	1 cup flavored bread crumbs

1 1/2 cups sundried tomatoes in oil, chopped
Salt and pepper to taste

Cook pasta according to directions or until al dente. In a small fry pan, add 2 tbsp of olive oil and bread crumbs and cook on low, stirring constantly until toasted. Remove and place to the side. In a large pan, add the oil, garlic and red pepper, cook until tender. Stir in the sundried tomatoes and cook for additional 3-5 minutes; remove from heat. Drain pasta and add to the oil mixture. Return to heat, stir in the basil, salt and pepper, toss to coat, and cook for 1 minute. Sprinkle with the toasted bread crumbs and serve.

BEFORE YOU BEGIN, REMEMBER TO EMPOWER YOUR HERB (see page 4)

ROASTED GARLIC AND SPINACH SALAD
Serves 4

12 large GARLIC cloves, unpeeled	1 lb spinach leaves
1/4 cup extra virgin olive oil	1 cup pecans, chopped
1 tbsp balsamic vinegar	Salt and pepper to taste
1 red onion, sliced thin	1 cup sliced mushrooms

8 slices cooked bacon, crumbled
8 oz shredded Swiss cheese

Preheat oven to 375. Place garlic in a small pan and toss with 2 tbsp oil; bake for 15 minutes until charred. Place the pecans on a tin and bake in the oven until toasted. While warm, add the garlic into a large bowl, add the spinach, onions, mushrooms, bacon, pecans and cheese. Add the vinegar and remaining oil, salt and pepper, and mix together. Squeeze out the softened garlic into your salad or spread on your favorite bread.

My name is MINT...
I hold the magical energy of GRATITUDE,
CONFIDENCE, HARMONY and SUPPORT...
I have a cool, soothing, sweet scent and
distinct, refreshing flavor.
My gift to you is FULFILLMENT...
Imagine that my energy surrounds you
and TRUST that you are SAFE and that
you are LOVED.

HERBS

CHICKEN SALAD WITH FRESH MINT
serves 4

4 boneless chicken breasts
1/2 cup fresh MINT finely chopped
1 small sweet onion, chopped
1/2 cup mayonnaise or to taste
1/4 cup walnuts chopped
1/4 cup grapes, finely chopped
salt and pepper to taste

Place chicken breast in a saucepan, add water to cover, and cook until done. Remove and let cool, then coarsely chop. In a large bowl, add the chicken, onion, mint, grapes, walnuts, salt, pepper and mayonnaise. Mix together and serve.

BEFORE YOU BEGIN, REMEMBER TO EMPOWER YOUR HERB (see page 4)

GRILLED LAMB CHOPS
serves 4

4 lamb chops
extra virgin olive oil
1 cup MINT, finely chopped
6 cloves garlic
salt and pepper to taste

Coat both sides of the chops with olive oil. Season with salt and pepper. For the garlic cloves, use a garlic press to get a paste-like consistency; then spread over both sides. Cover chops with mint and marinate for 2-3 hours. Remove mint before cooking. Grill chops to your desired taste and serve with a dollop of mint jelly.

My name is CILANTRO/CORIANDER..
I hold the magical energy of STRENGTH,
TENDERNESS, SUPPORT and COOPERATION...
Cilantro indicates my fresh leaves and
coriander refers to my seed. We are double
the pleasure yet distinctly individual.
My gift to you is BALANCE...
Imagine that my energy surrounds you
and TRUST that you are SAFE and that
you are LOVED.

HERBS

SOUTHWEST STIR-FRY
serves 4-6

6 boneless chicken breasts, cut into cubes
1 large onion, chopped
4 cloves garlic, chopped
3 tbsp extra virgin olive oil
1 tsp ground cumin
2 tbsp chili sauce
1/2 tbsp crushed red pepper or to taste
3 tbsp CILANTRO, finely chopped
4 oz canned or frozen corn
4 oz canned black beans
4 oz diced tomatoes
Salt and pepper to taste

In a large frying pan, add the oil, garlic and onion, and saute until tender. Add the chicken and cook until no longer pink. Add remaining ingredients and cook on medium/high heat for about 10-12 minutes, stirring constantly. Serve with white rice.

BEFORE YOU BEGIN, REMEMBER TO EMPOWER YOUR HERB (see page 4)

GUACAMOLE
serves 4

2 large ripe avocados
2 tomatoes, peeled & chopped
2 small white onions, finely chopped
2 small hot green chili peppers seeded & chopped
4 tbsp CILANTRO, finely chopped
2 tbsp lemon juice
5 tbsp light cream
Salt and pepper to taste

Cut the avocado in half and remove the pit. Scoop out the flesh and mash. Add the tomatoes, onion, chili peppers, cilantro, cream, lemon juice, salt and pepper. Stir to blend.

My name is SAGE...
I hold the magical energy of WISDOM, HOPE,
SELF ESTEEM and STRENGTH...
I have a very fragrant aroma and rich
powerful taste.
My gift to you is CONFIDENCE...
Imagine that my energy surrounds you and
TRUST that you are SAFE and that
you are LOVED.

HERBS

SAGE BURGERS
serves 4

1 1/2 lb chopped sirloin
1 onion, finely chopped
4 cloves garlic, finely chopped
1/4 cup fresh SAGE finely chopped (use less if dried)
2 - 3 tbsp Worcestershire sauce or to taste
salt and pepper to taste
4 thick cut slices of Swiss cheese
4 hamburger buns

In a large bowl, add the sirloin, onion, garlic, Worcestershire, sage, salt and pepper. Mix well and score into 4 sections. Shape into patties and grill or broil to your desired taste. Add the cheese at the very end of cooking. Serve with bun and favorite toppings.

BEFORE YOU BEGIN, REMEMBER TO EMPOWER YOUR HERB (see page 4)

OVEN FRIES WITH FRESH SAGE
serves 4

4 large baking potatoes, cut into wedges
Extra virgin olive oil
1/2 tbsp garlic powder
1/4 cup fresh SAGE finely chopped
Salt and pepper to taste

Preheat oven to 400. In a large bowl, add the potatoes, olive oil (just enough to coat), garlic powder, sage, salt and pepper. Mix together and place onto a baking pan. Bake until potatoes are golden brown.

My name is DILL...
I hold the magical energy of COMPASSION,
ACCEPTANCE, FAITH and PROTECTION...
My aromatic feathery green leaves have a
very subtle liquorice flavor.
My gift to you is VULNERABILITY...
Imagine that my energy surrounds you and
TRUST that you are SAFE and that
you are LOVED.

HERBS

TORTELLINI SALAD WITH FRESH DILL
Serves 6-8

16 oz frozen cheese tortellini
1/2 cup snipped fresh DILL
1 each green, red & yellow pepper, sliced
1 large sweet onion, thinly sliced
8 oz can black olives, coarsely chopped
4 plum tomatoes, chopped
1/2 tbsp garlic powder
3 tbsp extra virgin olive oil, or to taste
1-2 tbsp balsamic vinegar or to taste
Salt and pepper to taste

Cook tortellini according to directions, then cool in the fridge. In a large bowl, add the cooled tortellini, peppers, onion, olives, tomatoes, dill, salt, pepper, oil and balsamic vinegar. Mix well and serve.

BEFORE YOU BEGIN, REMEMBER TO EMPOWER YOUR HERB (see page 4)

SHRIMP SALAD WITH DILL BUTTERMILK DRESSING
Serves 4

16 oz baby cooked shrimp
2 celery sticks, finely chopped
1/2 cup slivered almonds

DILL BUTTERMILK DRESSING:
makes 2 cups

1 cup buttermilk	1/2 cup heavy cream
6 scallions, finely chopped	1/2 cup fresh DILL, chopped
2 garlic cloves, chopped	4 tbsp olive oil
2 tbsp lemon juice	Salt and pepper to taste

Make dressing ahead of time. Mix together all the dressing ingredients and blend in a food processor or blender. Chill for 1-2 hours or overnight. In a bowl, add the shrimp, celery, almonds and dill dressing; adjust amount according to taste. Mix together and serve on a bed of lettuce.

My name is BAY...
I hold the magical energy of COMFORT,
PURIFICATION, CLARITY and RELEASE...
I have glossy, dark leaves and a strong,
spicy flavor.
My gift to you is INTROSPECTION...
Imagine that my energy surrounds you and
TRUST that you are SAFE and that
you are LOVED.

HERBS

CHICKEN SOUP

1 small whole chicken
5-6 carrots, chopped
5 celery stalks, chopped
2 small or 1 large BAY leaf
1 large onion, chopped
1 10 oz bag fresh spinach
16 oz orzo or your favorite noodle
salt and pepper to taste

In a large pot, add the chicken and fill with water to cover. Add the carrots, celery, bay leaf, onion, salt and pepper. Let cook on low for 1 1/2 - 2 hours. When soup is ready, remove the chicken and place in the fridge to cool. Add the fresh spinach to the stock, stirring constantly until wilted. In a separate pot, cook the orzo according to directions. Leave the chicken out of the soup and use in the recipe below. Spoon orzo into a bowl, pour soup over orzo, remove bay leaf, and serve.

BEFORE YOU BEGIN, REMEMBER TO EMPOWER YOUR HERB (see page 4)

CHICKEN POT PIE
serves 4-6

2 deep dish frozen pie shells
1 box frozen mixed vegetables
1 can cream of chicken soup
1/2 tbsp garlic powder
Salt and pepper to taste
Cooled off chicken from soup

Remove chicken from the bone and cut into chucks. In a bowl, add the chicken, cream of chicken soup, mixed vegetables, garlic, salt and pepper. Mix well and spoon into pie shell. Use the second shell as the top pressing firmly down to close. Bake on 400 for about 30 minutes or until the crust is golden brown.

My name is ROSEMARY...
I hold the magical energy of
ENCOURAGEMENT, INTELLIGENCE, SECURITY
and FORGIVENESS...
I have a strong, woodsy aroma and
pungent, but pleasant taste.
My gift to you is CHOICE...
Imagine that my energy surrounds you
and TRUST that you are SAFE and that
you are LOVED.

HERBS

GRILLED STEAKS WITH ROSEMARY & GARLIC RUB
serves 4

4 sirloin steaks 4oz ea.
2 tbsp extra virgin olive oil
4 cloves garlic, finely chopped
2 tsp dried ROSEMARY
1/2 tsp sugar
salt and pepper to taste

Preheat grill to medium. In a bowl, combine the garlic, rosemary, sugar, salt and pepper. Pour the olive oil over the steaks, coating both sides. Rub the mixture onto the steaks and let marinate for 1 hour. Grill or broil steaks until your desired taste and serve.

BEFORE YOU BEGIN, REMEMBER TO EMPOWER YOUR HERB (see page 4)

OVEN ROASTED VEGETABLES
serves 4 - 6

2 baking potatoes, cut into chunks
2 sweet potatoes, cut into chunks
2 large zucchini, cut into chunks
1 large onion, chopped
8 oz mushrooms, chopped
3-4 carrots, cut into chunks
1/2 tbsp FRESH ROSEMARY, finely chopped
3 cloves garlic, finely chopped
1 stick butter, cut int sections
salt and pepper to taste

Preheat oven to 375. In a large baking pan, add all the ingredients and mix together. Bake for about 25-30 minutes or until vegetables are done.

SPICES

Sesame
Ginger
Nutmeg
Sea Salt
Caraway
Peppercorn
Cumin
Chili Pepper
Allspice
Mustard
Paprika
Sugarcane
Clove
Vanilla
Chocolate
Cinnamon

My is name is SESAME...
I hold the magical energy of DESIRE,
OPPORTUNITY, POWER and ABUNDANCE...
I have a very subtle aroma and
a wonderful nutty taste.
My gift to you is PROSPERITY...
Imagine that my energy surrounds you and
TRUST that you are SAFE and that
you are LOVED.

SPICES

SESAME STIR FRY
serves 4

4 boneless chicken breast, cut into strips
3-4 tbsp SESAME SEEDS, dry roasted

3 cloves garlic, chopped   1 onion, chopped
extra virgin olive oil   8 oz snow peas
3 carrots, cut into strips   2 red or green peppers
8 oz asparagus, cut into pieces   2-3 tbsp teriyaki sauce
2 cups cooked white rice   salt and pepper to taste

In a large frying pan, add the oil, enough to coat the bottom. On med/low heat, add the chicken, garlic and onion and cook until no longer pink. Add the snow peas, carrots, onion, asparagus, peppers, teriyaki, salt and pepper. Stir fry for about 10-12 minutes or until the vegetables are done. Cook rice according to directions. Toss stir-fry with roasted sesame seeds and serve over rice.

BEFORE YOU BEGIN, REMEMBER TO EMPOWER YOUR SPICE (see page 4)

BROCCOLI AND PASTA
Serves 4

16 oz frozen or fresh broccoli florets
4 garlic cloves., finely chopped
3 tbsp extra virgin olive oil
1/2 cup chicken stock
3-4 tbsp dry roasted SESAME SEEDS
16 oz linguine or favorite pasta
salt and pepper to taste

In a large pot, add the olive oil and garlic, and saute for a few minutes. Add the broccoli and saute an additional few minutes. Add chicken stock, salt and pepper, and bring to a boil, allowing the liquid to reduce a little, then remove from heat. Cook the pasta according to directions; drain and add to the broccoli. Mix together and sprinkle with roasted sesame seeds.

My name is GINGER...
I hold the magical energy of POTENTIAL,
SUCCESS, COMPASSION and CHOICE...
I have a refreshing aroma and a
spicy, warm flavor.
My gift to you is FORGIVENESS...
Imagine that my energy surrounds you
and TRUST that you are SAFE and that
you are LOVED.

SPICES

CHICKEN & PASTA STIR FRY WITH FRESH GINGER
Serves 4

1 lb boneless chicken breast, cut into cubes
3 tbsp olive oil
3 cloves garlic, finely chopped
1/4 inch fresh GINGER, peeled & sliced thin
2 bunches scallions, finely chopped
2 large green peppers
1/4 cup soy sauce
1 lb thin spaghetti
salt and pepper to taste

In a large frying pan, add 2 tbsp oil and the chicken, and cook on medium/low heat until no longer pink. Remove from pan and place in a bowl. Using the same pan, add the remaining oil, garlic and scallions and saute for a few minutes. Then add the peppers, ginger, salt and pepper and cook for about 5-7 minutes. Add the soy sauce and put the chicken back into the pan, allowing it to simmer for a few minutes. Cook pasta according to directions; then add to the pan. Mix well and serve.

BEFORE YOU BEGIN, REMEMBER TO EMPOWER YOUR SPICE (see page 4)

GRILLED ROAST PORK WITH GINGER GLAZE
Serves 4

1 1/2 lb pork roast   salt and pepper to taste
GINGER GLAZE: makes 1 cup
1 tbsp instant coffee   1/2 cup dry white wine
1/2 cup dark brown sugar   1 tsp ground GINGER
1/2 tsp Dijon mustard

Season pork with salt and pepper and cook according to specified weight. Beat together all the ingredients for the glaze. In a small pan, add glaze and simmer for 5-10 minutes. While glaze is still warm, brush over meat during the last 15 minutes of cooking. Let meat sit a few minutes; then slice and serve.

My name is NUTMEG...
I hold the magical energy of FAITH,
SUCCESS, POSSIBILITIES and PROSPERITY...
I have a beautiful, fragrant aroma and
a slightly sweet taste.
My gift to you is POTENTIAL...
Imagine that my energy surrounds you and
TRUST that you are SAFE and that
you are LOVED.

SPICES

CREAMY SPINACH SOUP
Serves 4

2 tbsp butter	1 onion, chopped
1 1/2 lb fresh spinach, chopped	5 cups chicken stock
2 oz creamed coconut	1/4 tsp NUTMEG
1 1/4 cups single cream	Salt and pepper to taste

Melt the butter in a saucepan over medium heat and saute the onion for a few minutes until soft. Add the spinach, cover and cook for 10 minutes until the spinach has reduced. Pour the spinach mixture into a blender or food processor and add a little stock. Blend until smooth. Return to the pan and add the remaining stock, creamed coconut, salt, pepper and nutmeg. Simmer for 15-20 minutes to thicken. Add the cream, stir well, and heat through; do not boil and serve hot.

BEFORE YOU BEGIN, REMEMBER TO EMPOWER YOUR SPICE (see page 4)

ANGEL HAIR PASTA WITH MUSHROOMS AND NUTMEG
Serves 4

4 tbsp butter	2 medium onions, chopped
4 cloves garlic, chopped	2 lbs mushrooms, sliced
1/4 tsp ground NUTMEG	1 cup heavy cream
1 lb angel hair pasta	salt and pepper to taste
2 tsp crushed red pepper	3 tbsp fresh parsley, chopped

In a large saucepan, heat the butter and add the onions and garlic. Cook over medium heat until onion is soft. Add the mushrooms, nutmeg, red pepper (optional), salt and pepper. Cook until mushrooms give up all their liquid. Add the cream and cook a few minutes longer. Cook pasta according to directions. Drain, and toss together the pasta, parsley and sauce. Serve with grated cheese.

My name is SEA SALT...
I hold the magical energy of CONFIDENCE,
OPTIMISM, DETERMINATION and
SIGNIFICANCE...
My role is threefold: I season, preserve and
provide nutrients necessary for your
body's function.
My gift to you is SELF WORTH...
I imagine that my energy surrounds you and
TRUST that you are SAFE and that
you are LOVED.

SPICES

FIVE STAR SPARE RIBS WITH SPICED SALT
Serves 4-6

10-12 spare ribs
vegetable oil for frying
2-3 tbsp flour

SPICY SALT:
1 tbsp SEA SALT
*1 tsp five spice powder

MARINADE:
2 tbsp soy sauce
1 tbsp brown sugar
3 cloves garlic, chopped
2 tbsp rice wine or dry sherry
1/2 tsp chili sauce
1 tsp crushed red pepper

Chop each rib into 3-4 pieces; mix all the marinade ingredients and marinate for at least 2 hours. Coat the ribs with flour and deep fry in medium hot oil until color is an even dark brown. * Five spice powder can be purchased or grind to a fine powder 1 tsp each of star anise, fennel seeds, cloves, cassia and Szechwan pepper. To make spicy salt, heat the salt and 1 tsp of the spice powder in a preheated pan for about 2 minutes over low heat, stirring constantly. Dip the ribs into the seasoning before serving.

BEFORE YOU BEGIN, REMEMBER TO EMPOWER YOUR SPICE (see page 4)

HERB SALT
Makes 1 lb

1 lb SEA SALT
4 bay leaves crumbled
2 tbsp dried rosemary
2 tbsp dried thyme
1 tsp dried oregano

SPICED SALT
Makes 1 lb

1 lb SEA SALT
2 tbsp cumin seeds
2 tbsp black peppercorns
1 tbsp coriander seeds
1 tsp cloves

Add all ingredients into a food processor. Mix until combined. Spoon into an air tight container for storage. Rub flavored salts into meat or fish before cooking. Use to season vegetables and sauces.

My name is CARAWAY...
I hold the magical energy of STABILITY,
CONNECTEDNESS, TRUTH and PROTECTION...
My seeds are warm and sweet with a
slightly, peppery aroma.
My gift to you is EMERGENCE...
Imagine that my energy surrounds you and
TRUST that you are SAFE and that
you are LOVED.

SPICES

SEED CAKE
Makes 9 inch cake

Butter & flour for preparing the pan
1 cup unsalted butter
1 cup plus 2 tbsp sugar
4 eggs
1 3/4 cups all purpose flour
1/2 tsp salt
1 tsp baking powder
1 tsp vanilla extract
1 tbsp CARAWAY seeds
1 cup cranberries or blueberries

Preheat the oven to 350. Grease and flour a 9 inch pan. In a bowl, cream together the butter and sugar until light and fluffy. Beat in one egg at a time. Add the flour, salt, and baking powder and add to butter mixture, blending thoroughly. Stir in the vanilla, fruit and caraway seeds, and pour into the prepared pan. Bake until the cake is golden and pulls away from the sides, about 50 minutes. Let cake stand 10 minutes before removing it from the pan. Serve plain or frosted with your favorite icing.

BEFORE YOU BEGIN, REMEMBER TO EMPOWER YOUR SPICE (see page 4)

SAUSAGE AND PEPPERS
Serves 4-6

3 lbs sausage, cut into pieces
2 1/2 lbs small red potatoes
2 tbsp extra virgin olive oil
8 oz mushrooms, chopped
4 cloves garlic, chopped
1/2 tbsp CARAWAY seeds
1 large onion, sliced
3 large green peppers, sliced
salt and pepper to taste

Preheat oven to 400. In a large baking pan, add the sausage, potatoes, peppers, onions, mushrooms, garlic, caraway, salt, pepper and olive oil. Mix together and bake for 1 hour or until sausage is golden brown.

My name is PEPPERCORN...
I hold the magical energy of SELF ESTEEM,
COURAGE, AUTHENTICITY and INITIATIVE...
I have a rich, earthy aroma and a highly
pungent, spicy taste.
My gift to you is RESPONSIBILITY...
Imagine that my energy surrounds you and
TRUST that you are SAFE and that
you are LOVED.

SPICES

PORK TENDERLOIN WITH ROASTED SALT AND PEPPER
Serves 4

1 lb pork tenderloin   5 whole cloves garlic
extra virgin olive oil   2 tbsp salt
             2 tsp BLACK PEPPER

Preheat oven to 350. Place tenderloin in a pan and make tiny openings in the skin with your knife; place the garlic into each one. Pour the olive oil over, coating both front and back. Cook for 30 minutes. Over a medium heat, add the salt and pepper into a pan stirring continuously until you smell the peppery aroma. Leave to cool. Remove tenderloin from the pan and roll in the roasted mixture, slice and serve.

BEFORE YOU BEGIN, REMEMBER TO EMPOWER YOUR SPICE (see page 4)

PEPPERED STEAK
Serves 4

4 filet mignons, 6 oz each   2 tbsp brandy
4 tbsp white PEPPERCORN   2 tbsp unsalted butter
2 tbsp black PEPPERCORN, crushed   Salt
1/2 cup heavy cream   1 cup beef stock or red wine

Reserve 1 tbsp white pepper and set aside. Spread the remaining white and black pepper on both sides of the steaks. In a skillet, heat the butter until foaming. Add the steaks and cook until brown on both sides, about 6-8 minutes or to desired taste. Transfer steaks to a plate and season with salt. Over a high heat, add the beef stock or red wine, scraping the bottom to remove any browned bits. Stir in the cream and brandy; bring to a boil. Add the reserved white pepper and cook until thickened, 2-3 minutes. Place steaks on individual plates. Pour sauce over and serve.

My name is CUMIN...
I hold the magical energy of FAITH,
BALANCE, PROTECTION and VALIDATION...
I am strong and spicy with a sweet aroma
and slightly pungent taste.
My gift to you is COOPERATION...
Imagine that my energy surrounds you
and TRUST that you are SAFE and that
you are LOVED.

SPICES

HOME-MADE HUMMUS
Makes 2 cups

1 can 19 oz chick-peas, drained & rinsed
1/2 cup plus 1 tbsp olive oil
1 1/2 tsp CUMIN
2 tbsp lemon juice
1 tbsp basil
3 tbsp sour cream

1 onion, chopped
1 tsp cayenne pepper
4 cloves garlic, chopped
salt and pepper to taste

In a pan, add the 1 tbsp oil, chick-peas, onion, cumin and cayenne pepper and cook over high heat for 1 minute. Transfer to a food processor, add the lemon juice, remaining olive oil, sour cream, basil, garlic, salt and pepper; then process until smooth.

BEFORE YOU BEGIN, REMEMBER TO EMPOWER YOUR SPICE (see page 4)

BLACK BEAN SOUP
Serves 4

1 can 19 oz black beans, rinsed & drained
1 green bell pepper
3 cloves garlic, minced
2 cups chicken broth
1 tsp coriander
sour cream

2 scallions, sliced
1 tbsp olive oil
1 tsp CUMIN
1/4 cup diced tomatoes

In a sauce pan, add the oil and saute the green pepper, scallions and garlic until soft. Add the black beans, chicken broth, coriander and cumin. Simmer for about 7 minutes. Remove half the beans and puree in a food processor or blender. Add back into the pan, stir and reheat. Serve with a dollop of sour cream.

My name is CHILI PEPPER...
I hold the magical energy of PASSION,
CHANGE, STIMULATION and ENTHUSIASM...
I have been known to have a chemical effect
on your body and can transform any bland
cuisine into a mouth tingling delight.
My gift to you is EXPRESSION...
Imagine that my energy surrounds you and
TRUST that you are SAFE and that
you are LOVED.

SPICES

PORK CHOPS WITH HOT PEPPERS
serves 4

8-10 boneless pork chops, medium to thin cut
16 oz jar hot banana PEPPERS in juice
4-6 large baking potatoes, peeled & sliced
4 cloves garlic, finely chopped
1/2 tbsp red wine or balsamic vinegar
2 tbsp olive oil   salt and pepper to taste

Over a medium heat, coat the bottom of a large sauce pan
with the olive oil. Add the chopped garlic and pork chops.
Allow the chops to get white on both sides, about 2-3 minutes.
Add the potatoes, vinegar, the jar of peppers and all the juice
in the jar. Salt and pepper to taste. Stir to mix and cook over
medium to low heat for about 1 hour or until the chops and
potatoes are tender.

BEFORE YOU BEGIN, REMEMBER TO EMPOWER YOUR SPICE (see page 4)

TURKEY CHILI NACHOS
serves 4

1 1/4 lb chopped turkey breast (can use beef or pork)
28 oz can crushed tomatoes   15 oz can kidney beans
1 large onion, chopped   2 tbsp CHILI POWDER
2 tsp crushed red pepper   1 tsp ground cumin
1/2 tbsp garlic powder   1/2 tsp oregano
12 oz colby jack cheese, shredded   salt to taste
2 tbsp oil   1 large bag nachos

In a large sauce pan, add the oil and turkey and cook until
no longer pink. Add the crushed tomatoes, kidney beans,
onion and all the dry ingredients. Mix well and cook on
medium to low for about 30 minutes. Place the nachos on a
pan and layer the nachos with chili and cheese; keep
repeating until done. Put under the broiler until cheese is
melted and serve.

My name is ALLSPICE...
I hold the magical energy of COMFORT,
SPONTANEITY, FREEDOM and PLEASURE...
My name describes my flavor which is a
combination of nutmeg, cinnamon and
cloves. I am a versatile spice that can be
used in both sweet and savory dishes.
My gift to you is WILLINGNESS...
Imagine that my energy surrounds you
and TRUST that you are SAFE and that
you are LOVED.

SPICES

ALLSPICE SHRIMP AND RICE
Serves 4-6

3 tbsp extra virgin olive oil
2 medium onion, chopped
3 cups beer
3 cloves garlic, chopped
1 1/4 tsp crushed ALLSPICE
2 cups cooked rice
1 1/2-2 lb shrimp, peeled & deveined
salt and pepper to taste

In a large saucepan, add 2 tbsp oil, 2 cloves garlic and 1 onion; saute until tender. Add the beer, 1 tsp allspice, salt and pepper, and simmer for 10 minutes. Allow the beer to reduce a little. Add the shrimp and cook until done. Remove shrimp from the pan. In a small fry pan, add 1 tbsp oil and remaining onion and garlic; saute until tender. Add the cooked rice, 1/4 tsp allspice, salt and pepper. Stir and saute a few minutes. Top with shrimp and serve.

BEFORE YOU BEGIN, REMEMBER TO EMPOWER YOUR SPICE (see page 4)

FRESH GREEN BEANS WITH ALLSPICE
serves 4

1 1/2 lb fresh green beans
1/2 tsp crushed ALLSPICE
salt and pepper to taste

8 slices bacon
3 cloves garlic, chopped

Clean and trim green beans. In a large frying pan, cook the bacon until crisp. Remove bacon and place on the side. Over medium heat, add the garlic to the bacon drippings and saute for a few minutes. Add the green beans, allspice, salt and pepper; stir, cover, and cook until beans are tender. Crumble up the bacon, toss with the green beans and serve.

My name is MUSTARD...
I hold the magical energy of PERCEPTION,
IMAGINATION, SERENITY and FOCUS...
Although my seeds have no smell, my spicy
flavor will undeniably tingle your
taste buds.
My gift to you is AWARENESS...
Imagine that my energy surrounds you and
TRUST that you are SAFE and that
you are LOVED.

SPICES

CAJUN SPICE MIX

1 tsp black peppercorns	1 tsp cumin seeds
1tsp MUSTARD seeds	2 tsp paprika
1 tsp chilli powder	1 tsp dried oregano
1 tsp dried thyme	1 tsp salt
2 garlic cloves	1 med onion, sliced

Dry fry the peppercorns, cumin and mustard seed over a medium heat unil you can smell their flavor. Grind the spices in a food processor to a fine powder; then add the paprika, chili powder, oregano, thyme and salt, and grind again. If it is to be used immediately, add the spices, garlic and onion into a food processor and mix until well combined. Add entire quantity to the recipe below.

> BEFORE YOU BEGIN, REMEMBER TO EMPOWER YOUR SPICE (see page 4)

JAMBALAYA
serves 4

2 tbsp oil	
8 oz chicken, cubed	8 oz chorizo sausage, cubed
3 celery sticks, chopped	2 1/2 cups chicken stock
1 red & green pepper, seeded and chopped	
1 quantity of cajun spice mix (see recipe above)	
1 cup long grain rice	8 oz can chopped tomatoes

Heat the oil in a large frying pan. Fry the chicken and sausage until lightly browned. Remove from the pan and set aside. Add the celery and peppers and fry for 2-3 minutes. Return the chicken and sausage to the pan. Stir in the cajun spice mix and cook for 2-3 minutes. Stir in the rice and add the tomatoes and stock. Bring to a boil and stir. Turn the heat to low, cover the pan, and simmer gently for 15-20 minutes until the rice is tender and the liquid has been absorbed.

My name is PAPRIKA...
I hold the magical energy of FULFILLMENT,
CLARITY, GENTLENESS and SINCERITY...
I am a beautiful deep red color. My sweet
taste is an excellent source of vitamin C.
My gift to you is WHOLENESS...
Imagine that my energy surrounds you and
TRUST that you are SAFE and that
you are LOVED.

SPICES

TURKEY MEATLOAF
serves 4-6

1 1/4 lbs chopped turkey breast (can use beef or pork)
1 egg
1 cup flavored bread crumbs
4 oz can tomato sauce
8 oz chopped mushrooms
1/2 tbsp PAPRIKA
1 medium onion, chopped
4 cloves garlic, chopped
salt and pepper to taste

Preheat oven to 375. Mix together turkey, bread crumbs, mushrooms, egg, onion, garlic, paprika, salt, pepper and tomato sauce. Place into a baking pan and form into a loaf. Before placing in the oven, add about 1/2 inch water on the bottom of the pan and cook for 1 hour.

BEFORE YOU BEGIN, REMEMBER TO EMPOWER YOUR SPICE (see page 4)

PAPRIKA MASHED POTATOES
serves 4-6

2 lbs peeled and sliced baking potatoes.
6 cloves garlic
1/3 cup butter
3/4 cup sour cream
1 tsp PAPRIKA
salt and pepper to taste

In a saucepan of boiling water, cook potatoes and garlic until tender. Drain and mash with butter, sour cream, paprika, salt and pepper.

My name is SUGARCANE...
I hold the magical energy of EXPRESSION,
CONTENTMENT, JOY and GRATITUDE...
My strong, sweet taste comes in a variety of
forms. I am a tropical plant and one of the
oldest culinary flavorings.
My gift to you is SATISFACTION...
Imagine that my energy surrounds you
and TRUST that you are SAFE and that
you are LOVED.

SPICES

BUTTER BALLS

2 cups butter, softened
8 tbsp SUGAR
4 cups flour
2 tsp vanilla
2 tsp baking powder
1/2 cup chopped walnuts
confectionery SUGAR to coat

Preheat oven to 350. Mix together the butter, sugar, flour, vanilla, baking powder and walnuts. Form into small balls and place on a baking sheet. Bake for 15 minutes. While cookies are still warm, roll in confectionery sugar to coat. Makes approximately 30 cookies.

BEFORE YOU BEGIN, REMEMBER TO EMPOWER YOUR SPICE (see page 4)

CHEESE CAKE

9 inch spring form pan
1 1/4 cup graham cracker crumbs
6 tbsp unsalted butter, melted
6 8 oz cream cheese, softened
1/4 tsp grated lemon rind

3 tbsp SUGAR
8 eggs
2 tsp vanilla
2 cups SUGAR

Preheat oven to 375. Mix together the crumbs, butter and 3 tbsp sugar. Press the mixture into the bottom of the spring form pan and bake for 10 minutes or until golden. Remove and lower heat to 300. Beat together the cream cheese and sugar. Then add one egg at a time. Beat each egg into mixture before adding the next. Add the vanilla and lemon mix and pour into pan. Place the spring form pan into a larger pan filled with about 1 inch of water. Bake for 1 1/2 hours. Remove from pan of water and let cool.

SPICES

My name is CLOVE...
I hold the magical energy of
TRANSFORMATION, GROWTH, WELL-BEING
and ENCOURAGEMENT...
I have a strong and fiery aroma with a
sweet and pungent taste.
My gift to you is RENEWAL...
Imagine that my energy surrounds you and
TRUST that you are SAFE and that
you are LOVED.

SPICES

LEMON ICED TEA
Serves 6

7 1/2 cups cold water
8-10 CLOVES
1 cinnamon stick
juice of 2 lemons
6 tbsp sugar or to taste
6-8 mint leaves
4 Earl Grey, Lapsang or favorite tea bags
lemon or orange slices

Place all the ingredients in a container. Cover tightly and place in the fridge overnight or at least until the flavors infuse. Strain into glasses and serve decorated with lemon or orange slices.

BEFORE YOU BEGIN, REMEMBER TO EMPOWER YOUR SPICE (see page 4)

SPICED COFFEE
Serves 4

4 cups freshly made black coffee
4 cinnamon sticks
6 CLOVES
3-4 tbsp sugar or to taste
4 tbsp coffee liqueur
ice cubes

Pour the coffee into a large bowl. Add the cinnamon, cloves and sugar. Stir well and leave for at least 1 hour. Strain the coffee into a large jug; add the liqueur, ice ,and serve.

My name is VANILLA...
I hold the magical energy of PLEASURE,
HAPPINESS, EXCITEMENT and
STIMULATION...
I have a sweet, exotic aroma and a rich,
mellow taste.
My gift to you is SENSUALITY...
Imagine that my energy surrounds you
and TRUST that you are SAFE and that
you are LOVED.

SPICES

VANILLA CUSTARD SAUCE
Makes about 2 cups

4 large egg yolks, beaten
1/3 cup sugar
pinch of salt
2 cups heavy cream, scalded
1 tsp VANILLA extract
2 cups fresh mixed berries or favorite fruit
16 vanilla wafers

Beat the egg yolks with the sugar and salt in a large bowl until light and foamy. Heat the heavy cream just until it bubbles, then pour it into the egg yolks and beat together. Transfer the mixture to the top of a double boiler over barely simmering water. Cook, stirring constantly, until the mixture coats the spoon, about 8 minutes. Remove the sauce from the heat and stir in the vanilla and allow the sauce to cool. Using 4 martini glasses, line up 4 wafers in each glass, pressing down to fit. Spoon some fruit in the bottom, then custard, more fruit, another scoop of custard; top with whipped cream and a couple pieces of fresh berries.

BEFORE YOU BEGIN, REMEMBER TO EMPOWER YOUR SPICE *(see page 4)*

ICED CHOCOLATE & VANILLA INDULGENCE
Serves 4

4 tbsp coco powder   *1 3/4 cups single cream*
1/2 tsp VANILLA   *4 scoops of VANILLA ice cream*

In a small pan, add the coco powder and 1 cup of the cream. Heat gently, stirring until almost boiling, then remove pan from heat. Pour hot chocolate into bowl and mix in the remaining milk and vanilla. Pour mixture into 4 tall glasses, filling them 3/4 of the way. Top each one with a scoop of ice cream. Garnish with mint.

My name is CHOCOLATE...
I hold the magical energy of SENSUALITY,
SPIRITUAL WISDOM, PASSION and
INTIMACY...
I am known as the "food of the Gods". I have
a smooth texture and a rich powerful taste.
My gift to you is PLEASURE...
Imagine that my energy surrounds you
and TRUST that you are SAFE and that
you are LOVED.

SPICES

CHOCOLATE BROWNIES
Makes 16

6 oz CHOCOLATE, chopped into small pieces
1/2 cup vegetable oil   1 1/4 cups sugar
2 eggs   1 tsp vanilla
1/2 cup flour   4 tbsp COCOA powder
3/4 cups pecans, chopped   6 oz milk CHOCOLATE chips
1 can dark CHOCOLATE frosting

Preheat the oven to 350. Grease a 7 1/2 inch cake tin. Melt the chocolate in metal bowl over a saucepan of boiling water. In a large bowl, beat the oil, sugar, eggs and vanilla together. Stir in the melted chocolate and mix until smooth. Add the flour, cocoa powder, nuts and chocolate chips. Mix well and spread mixture evenly to the edges of the pan. Bake for 30-35 minutes or until firm and crusty. After brownies are cool, spread the dark chocolate frosting over the top and cut into bars.

BEFORE YOU BEGIN, REMEMBER TO EMPOWER YOUR SPICE (see page 4)

CHOCOLATE FONDUE
Makes about 1 1/2 cups

2/3 cup light corn syrup
1/2 cup heavy cream
8 oz semisweet CHOCOLATE chips

In a sauce pan over medium heat, bring the corn syrup and cream to a boil. Remove the pan from the heat and beat in the chocolate until it is melted. Dip any of your favorite fruits, pretzels, potato chips, cakes or cookies into the warm sauce.

My name is CINNAMON...
I hold the magical energy of PEACE,
KINDNESS, SERENITY and VALIDATION...
I have a delightful fragrance and a
sweet warm flavor.
My gift to you is WELL-BEING...
Imagine that my energy surrounds you
and TRUST that you are SAFE and that
you are LOVED.

SPICES

CRUMB CAKE
13X9 baking dish

1 box moist deluxe yellow cake mix
2 1/2 sticks butter, softened & cut up into sections
3 cups flour
1 cup sugar
2 tbsp CINNAMON

Preheat oven to 375. Prepare cake mix according to directions and bake. In a bowl, combine the flour, sugar and cinnamon; then add the butter. Mix until it holds together and forms crumbs. 10 minutes before cake is done, remove from the oven. Sprinkle crumb mixture over the top, covering thoroughly, and bake for 10 minutes. Remove and cool.

BEFORE YOU BEGIN, REMEMBER TO EMPOWER YOUR SPICE (see page 4)

APPLE CINNAMON ALA MODE
Serves 4

4 martini glasses
1 can apple pie filling
2 tbsp CINNAMON
vanilla ice cream
12 short bread cookies

Line up 3 cookies in each glass. Mix together the pie filling and 1 tbsp of cinnamon; microwave until warm. Spoon filling into the bottom of each glass and top with scoop of ice cream. Sprinkle with remaining cinnamon and serve.

VEGETABLES

Carrots
Celery
Corn
Potatoes
Peas
Onions
Lettuce
Cucumbers
Cabbage
Broccoli
Spinach

My name is CARROT...
I hold the magical energy of WISDOM,
CREATIVITY, SELF WORTH and BALANCE...
I have a clean, fresh, sweet taste and provide
large amounts of essential vitamins and
minerals.
My gift to you is INNER POWER...
Imagine that my energy surrounds you and
TRUST that you are SAFE and that
you are LOVED.

CARROT CAKE

FROSTING
1 cup softened cream cheese
2 1/4 tbsp softened butter
2 cups confectionery sugar

2 8-inch round tins	3 eggs
1 cup vegetable oil	1 1/2 cup flour
1 1/2 tsp baking powder	1 1/2 tsp baking soda
1 tsp salt	1 1/2 tsp ground cinnamon
pinch of nutmeg	1/4 tsp ground ginger

1 cup chopped walnuts
1/2 cup golden raisins, chopped

8 oz shredded CARROTS	1 tsp vanilla
2 heaping tbsp sour cream	1/2 cup sugar
1/2 cup light brown sugar	

BEFORE YOU BEGIN, REMEMBER TO EMPOWER YOUR VEGETABLE (see page 4)

Preheat oven to 350. Grease the pans and line them with wax paper. In a large bowl, combine the oil and sugar and mix well. Add the eggs one at a time and beat into the mixture. Add the flour, baking powder and soda, salt, cinnamon, nutmeg, ginger, and mix well. Fold in the walnuts, carrots, vanilla and sour cream. Divide mixture between pans and bake for 1 hour. Let cake cool.

FROSTING: Mix together the cream cheese, confectionery sugar and butter until smooth. Remove cooled cakes from pans. Spread frosting on one half and place the other on top. Spread the remaining frosting all over cake covering thoroughly.

My name is CELERY...
I hold the magical energy of POWER,
PASSION, INTROSPECTION and PURPOSE...
I have a crunchy texture and a distinct,
sharp taste.
My gift to you is SPIRITUAL WISDOM...
Imagine that my energy surrounds you and
TRUST that you are SAFE and that
you are LOVED.

VEGETABLES

CRAB SALAD WITH CHOPPED CELERY
Serves 4

2 CELERY sticks, finely chopped
1 lb crab meat
1/4 tsp ground ginger
1/2 tsp ground coriander
1 tsp garlic powder
1/4 cup mayonnaise
2 tbsp sour cream
1 tbsp lemon juice
salt and pepper to taste
a couple dashes of tabasco sauce
1 apple, chopped
1/2 cup chopped walnuts
1/4 cup parsley, chopped

In a large bowl, combine the coriander, ginger, mayonnaise, sour cream, lemon juice, salt, pepper, tabasco, crab meat, apple, parsley and walnuts. Mix well and serve with your favorite bread, crackers or salad.

BEFORE YOU BEGIN, REMEMBER TO EMPOWER YOUR VEGETABLE (see page 4)

STUFFED CELERY

12 CELERY sticks (leave the leaf on)
1/2 cup blue cheese or gorgonzola
1/2 cup cream cheese, softened
1/4 cup chopped chives

In a small bowl, mash the cheese and chives together until smooth. Fill the celery with the cheese mixture. Chill for 30-40 minutes and serve.

My name is CORN...
I hold the magical energy of SUCCESS,
HAPPINESS, FREEDOM and CONFIDENCE...
The native Indians referred to me as the "source
of life". My husks are green with golden tassels
and my taste deliciously sweet.
My gift to you is GOOD FORTUNE...
Imagine that my energy surrounds you and
TRUST that you are SAFE and that
you are LOVED.

VEGETABLES

CREAMED CORN FRITTERS
Makes about 20

1 12-oz can creamed CORN
5 Almonds
2 cloves garlic
1 small onion, chopped
1/2 inch piece of ginger, peeled & sliced
1 tsp coriander
1 red bell pepper, finely chopped
3 tbsp extra virgin olive oil
3 eggs, beaten
2 tbsp coconut
1/2 cup parsley, finely chopped
2 spring onions, finely chopped
Salt and pepper to taste

BEFORE YOU BEGIN, REMEMBER TO EMPOWER YOUR VEGETABLE (see page 4)

Grind in a food processor the almonds, garlic, onion, ginger and coriander to a fine paste. Heat 1 tbsp oil in a pan and fry paste for about 3-4 minutes. In a large bowl, add the beaten eggs, fried spices, coconut, spring onions, red pepper, parsley, salt, pepper and creamed corn. Mix well and heat the remaining oil. Drop large spoonfuls of the mixture into the pan and fry until golden brown and crispy on both sides. Serve with a side of sour cream and chives.

My name is POTATO...
I hold the magical energy of CHANGE,
HEALING, SUPPORT and WELL - BEING...
My firm, creamy flesh has a very
distinctive flavor and is also an excellent
source of vitamin C.
My gift to you is TRANSFORMATION...
Imagine that my energy surrounds you and
TRUST that you are SAFE and that
you are LOVED.

VEGETABLES

POTATO AND EGG OMELET
Serves 4-6

12 large eggs
2 green peppers, chopped
1 medium onion, chopped
1 large baking POTATO, peeled and chopped
1/2 cup milk or cream
2 tbsp extra virgin olive oil
1 tsp garlic powder
salt and pepper to taste

In a large frying pan, add the oil, peppers, potatoes, onions, salt, pepper and garlic and cook on low until potatoes are tender. In a bowl, add the eggs and cream; season to taste and beat well. When vegetables are done, add the eggs and stir to mix. Cook on low until bottom is set. Then place under a broiler for just a few minutes to cook top. Slide out from pan and serve. If your handle is not heat-proof, wrap tin foil around the handle to protect before putting into the oven.

BEFORE YOU BEGIN, REMEMBER TO EMPOWER YOUR VEGETABLE (see page 4)

POTATO AND ONION WITH OREGANO

5-lb bag red POTATOES, cut in half (leave skin on)
1 large sweet onion, chopped
3 cloves garlic, choppped
1 stick butter, cut into sections
2 tbsp dried oregano
salt and pepper to taste

Preheat oven to 375. In a large baking pan, add the potatoes, onions, garlic, oregano, salt, pepper and butter. Mix together and bake for 20-30 minutes or until potatoes are tender.

My name is PEA...
I hold the magical energy of LOVE,
WISHES, PROSPERITY and ENCOURAGEMENT...
I have a bright green pod and a delicate,
fresh flavor.
My gift to you is ATTRACTION...
Imagine that my energy surrounds you and
TRUST that you are SAFE and that
you are LOVED.

VEGETABLES

PEAS AND MACARONI
Serves 4-6

1 lb ditilini pasta
3 cloves garlic, chopped
1 small onion, chopped
1 tbsp olive oil
2 tsp crushed red pepper (optional)
2 cups frozen or canned PEAS
28 oz can crushed tomatoes
1/2 cup water
salt and pepper to taste

In large saucepan, add the oil, onions, garlic and saute until tender. Add the peas, tomatoes, red pepper, salt and pepper; stir and cook on med/low for about 30 minutes. Cook pasta according to directions, drain and add to sauce. Mix well and serve.

BEFORE YOU BEGIN, REMEMBER TO EMPOWER YOUR VEGETABLE (see page

ONE POT SPICY CHICKEN
Serves 4-6

1 lb boneless chicken breasts, cubed	1 onion, chopped
2 cloves garlic, chopped	2 tbsp oil
2 oz pepperoni, chopped	2 1/2 cups water
1 large green pepper, chopped	10 oz saffron rice
1 cup frozen PEAS	4 oz pimentos, chopped

In a large saucepan, add the oil, chicken, onion, garlic, and saute until no longer pink. Stir in the water and bring to a boil. Add the rice, pepper and pepperoni. Lower heat and simmer for 20 minutes or until rice is done. Add the peas and pimiento and cook an additional 1 minute and serve.

My Name is ONION...
I hold the magical energy of DESIRE,
PROTECTION, ABUNDANCE and CLARITY...
I come in a variety of different colors and
strengths and have a unique, savory flavor.
My gift to you is HOPE...
Imagine that my energy surrounds you
and TRUST that you are SAFE and that
you are LOVED.

VEGETABLES

ORZO WITH SAUTED ONION AND MUSHROOMS
Serves 6-8

1/2 lb orzo
4 cups chicken stock (2 cans)
1/2 stick butter
1 medium sweet ONION, finely chopped
3 cloves garlic, chopped
2 portabella mushrooms, chopped
8 oz chopped fresh spinach
salt and pepper to taste

In a sauce pan, add the chicken stock and bring to a boil. Then add the orzo and cook until all the liquid is absorbed. Keep an eye on it, constantly stirring or it may stick and burn. In a large frying pan, add the butter, onions, garlic and saute until tender. Add the mushrooms, salt and pepper, and stir. Cook an additional 5 minutes. When orzo is done, add to mixture and stir in spinach until wilted. Remove from the heat and serve.

BEFORE YOU BEGIN, REMEMBER TO EMPOWER YOUR VEGETABLE (see page

ONION SAUCE

4 large sweet ONIONS, sliced
8 oz tomato sauce
1/3 cup catsup

3 tbsp oil
2 tbsp spicy brown mustard
Salt and pepper to taste

In a large skillet, add the oil and onions, saute until tender. Add the tomato sauce, mustard, catsup, salt and pepper stir and cook for 10 minutes. Serve as a topping to hot dogs, hamburgers or sausage.

My name is LETTUCE...
I hold the magical energy of PEACE,
APPRECIATION, SECURITY and
COMPASSION...
I have a refreshing taste and a firm,
crunchy texture. I am also an excellent
source of vitamins and minerals.
My gift to you is TRANQUILITY...
Imagine that my energy surrounds you and
TRUST that you are SAFE and that
you are LOVED.

VEGETABLES

LETTUCE WRAPS

1 head iceberg LETTUCE
1 1/4 lbs chopped turkey or chicken breast
3 scallions, finely chopped
3 cloves garlic, chopped
1 cup chopped roasted peanuts
2 tbsp oil
2 tbsp worcestershire sauce
2 tsp crushed red pepper (optional)
3 tbsp teriyaki sauce
salt and pepper to taste

In a large frying pan, add the oil, garlic, scallions and chopped meat. Cook until no longer pink. Add the worcestershire sauce, teriyaki, red pepper, salt and pepper. Stir and cook on low for 5 - 10 minutes. Separate the lettuce leaves and spoon mixture onto each leaf. Top with peanuts and roll up.

BEFORE YOU BEGIN, REMEMBER TO EMPOWER YOUR VEGETABLE (see page 4)

CHOPPED SALAD WITH CREAMY ITALIAN DRESSING

4 oz chopped Spanish olives
6 cups romaine LETTUCE
1 small red onion, sliced thin
4 oz cheddar or blue cheese

4 oz artichoke hearts
3 plum tomatoes, chopped
1 cucumber, sliced
croutons, for topping

DRESSING

1 cup mayonnaise
2 tbsp white wine vinegar
1 tbsp dried oregano

1/4 cup heavy cream
1 clove garlic, chopped
salt and pepper to taste

Beat together all the ingredients for the dressing and chill for 1 hour. Prepare the salad and pour dressing over and toss. Top with croutons.

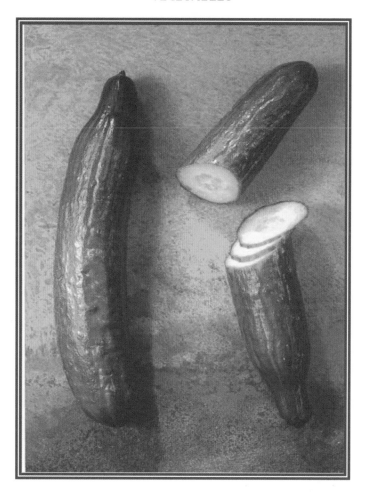

My name is CUCUMBER...
I hold the magical energy of PURIFICATION,
RENEWAL, POSSIBILITIES and CHANGE...
I have a refreshing taste and a cool,
crisp texture.
My gift to you is NEW BEGINNINGS...
Imagine that my energy surrounds you and
TRUST that you are SAFE and that
you are LOVED.

VEGETABLES

CUCUMBER SALAD
Serves 4

1 can black olives, chopped
1 large CUCUMBER, finely chopped
1 red bell pepper, finely chopped
4 plum tomatoes, chopped
1 small red onion, thinly sliced
5 basil leaves, finely chopped
2 garlic cloves, crushed
5 tbsp extra virgin olive oil
1 1/2 -2 tbsp red wine vinegar
salt and pepper to taste
1 loaf Italian or French bread

In a large bowl, add the cucumber, pepper, olives, onion, tomatoes and basil. In a small bowl add the garlic, oil, vinegar, salt and pepper and mix well. Pour over salad and toss. Warm the bread in the oven and serve.

BEFORE YOU BEGIN, REMEMBER TO EMPOWER YOUR VEGETABLE (see page 4)

SALMON CUCUMBER BITS
Makes about 40

4 seedless CUCUMBERS, thickly sliced
1 tbsp cilantro, finely chopped
8 oz cream cheese, softened   1 tbsp chives, chopped
7 oz can salmon, drained   2 tsp fresh thyme, chopped
1 tbsp sour cream   1 tbsp mayonnaise
1-2 tsp lemon juice   salt and pepper to taste

In a large bowl, add the cream cheese, salmon, sour cream, mayonnaise, lemon juice, cilantro, chives, thyme, salt and pepper. Mix until combined. Arrange sliced cucumbers on a platter, spread mixture on each one, and serve.

My name is CABBAGE...
I hold the magical energy of LUCK,
PROSPERITY, EXPRESSION and POTENTIAL...
I have pale green leaves and a slightly
pointed head. When cooked long and slow
I have a mild, pleasant flavor.
My gift to you is SUCCESS...
Imagine that my energy surrounds you and
TRUST that you are SAFE and that
you are LOVED.

VEGETABLES

TENDERLOIN AND CABBAGE
Serves 4

2 1/2 - 3 lbs pork butt
1 large head of CABBAGE, chopped
6 large baking potatoes, peeled and cut into chunks
salt and pepper to taste

In a large pot, add the tenderloin and cover with water.
Cook for 1 hour. Add the cabbage, potatoes, salt and pepper
and cook for 1 hour or until the potatoes are tender.

BEFORE YOU BEGIN, REMEMBER TO EMPOWER YOUR VEGETABLE (see page 4)

STUFFED CABBAGE
Serves 4-6

1 head CABBAGE, cored
2 cups cooked rice
1 lb chopped beef
1 tbsp garlic powder
3 16-oz cans tomato sauce
1 cup pitted prunes
salt and pepper to taste

In a large saucepan, add the head of cabbage and cover
with water to the top. Cook for 20 minutes on low. Mix
together the cooked rice, chopped meat, 1/2 tbsp garlic
powder, salt and pepper. Drain cabbage and peel its leaves.
Spoon mixture onto the leaf, roll up, and place into the
saucepan. In a bowl, mix together the tomato sauce,
remaining garlic, pitted prunes, salt and pepper, and pour
over cabbage. Cook on medium for 1 hour.

My name is BROCCOLI...
I hold the magical energy of
HUMOR, STIMULATION, ENRICHMENT
and HAPPINESS...
I am one of the most popular vegetables. My
large, green head and firm, succulent stalks
have a very pleasing flavor.
My gift to you is LAUGHTER...
Imagine that my energy surrounds you and
TRUST that you are SAFE and that
you are LOVED.

VEGETABLES

BROCCOLI WITH GARLIC & OIL
Serves 4

2 10-oz frozen or fresh BROCCOLI
4 large cloves garlic, chopped
3 tbsp extra virgin olive oil
salt and pepper to taste

In a saucepan, add water and broccoli and cook until crisp /tender. Drain broccoli and place to the side. Add the oil and garlic to the pan and saute on low for a few minutes, allowing the oil to infuse. Add back the broccoli, salt and pepper. Stir and cook a few minutes longer. Remove and serve.

BEFORE YOU BEGIN, REMEMBER TO EMPOWER YOUR VEGETABLE (see page 4)

CHICKEN AND BROCCOLI
Serves 4

4 boneless chicken breasts, cut into strips
6 cups BROCCOLI florets
3 cloves garlic, chopped
1 medium red onion
4 tbsp olive oil
1 large red bell pepper, sliced thin
1/4 cup chicken stock
1/4 cup soy sauce
salt and pepper to taste

In a large frying pan, add 2 tbsp of oil and the chicken. Cook until no longer pink. Remove and place to the side. Add remaining oil, garlic, onion, pepper and broccoli, and saute a few minutes. Then add stock, soy sauce, salt, pepper and the chicken back into the pan. Simmer for about 10 minutes.   Serve with your favorite rice.

My name is SPINACH...
I hold the magical energy of COURAGE,
TRUTH, COMPLETION and DETERMINATION...
My delicious, emerald green leaves are
extremely healthy and offer a rich balance
of flavor.
My gift to you is WILL - POWER...
Imagine that my energy surrounds you and
TRUST that you are SAFE and that
you are LOVED.

VEGETABLES

SPINACH AND CANNELLINI BEANS
Serves 4

2 10-oz packages frozen SPINACH, thawed & drained
3 cloves garlic, chopped
extra virgin olive oil (enough to coat bottom of pan)
1 15-oz can cannellini beans, drained
salt and pepper to taste

In a large frying pan, add the oil and garlic and saute for
a few minutes. Add the spinach, beans, salt and pepper, and
cook on low for about 25-30 minutes.
Serve with your favorite crusty bread.

BEFORE YOU BEGIN, REMEMBER TO EMPOWER YOUR VEGETABLE (see page 4)

SPINACH DIP
Makes 3 cups

1 10-oz package frozen SPINACH, thawed & squeezed dry
8 oz sour cream
1 cup mayonnaise
8 oz shredded cheddar or Swiss cheese
1 packet dry vegetable soup mix
8 oz chopped walnuts

Preheat oven to 375. In a 1 quart casserole, mix together 4
oz cheese, sour cream, mayonnaise, soup mix, spinach and
walnuts. Spoon into casserole and sprinkle remaining cheese
over the top. Bake until cheese is melted. Serve with your
favorite chips, breads
and vegetable.

FRUITS

Strawberries
Blueberries
Pears
Apples
Cherries
Oranges
Pineapples
Peaches
Raspberries
Plums
Plantains
Limes
Lemons
Grapes
Bananas
Tomatoes
Nuts
Coconuts

FRUITS

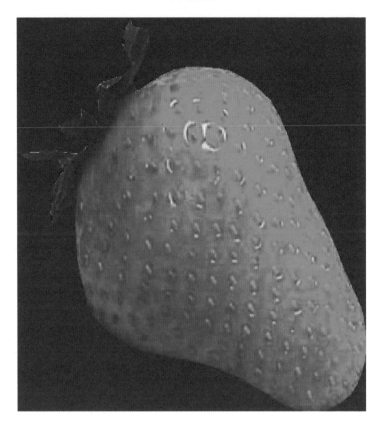

My name is STRAWBERRY...
I hold the magical energy of LOVE,
SENSUALITY, GOOD FORTUNE and
ATTRACTION...
I have beautiful, red skin and a juicy,
sweet flavor.
My gift to you is PASSION...
Imagine that my energy surrounds you and
TRUST that you are SAFE and that
you are LOVED.

FRUITS

STRAWBERRY SHORT CAKES
Serves 6

2 cups fresh STRAWBERRIES
1 package mini short cakes
1 cup heavy cream, chilled
2 tbsp confectioner's sugar

Beat the cream and sugar on high speed until peaks form. (Makes about 2 cups). Rinse and cut up strawberries. If berries are not sweet enough, add 1 tbsp sugar and mix to coat. Spoon into short cakes and top with whipped cream.

BEFORE YOU BEGIN, REMEMBER TO EMPOWER YOUR FRUIT (see page 4)

CHOCOLATE COVERED STRAWBERRIES

1 lb fresh STRAWBERRIES, rinsed and dried
12 oz chocolate, chopped

Add the chocolate to a heat-proof bowl and place over pot of barely simmering water until melted. Dip strawberries in and place on a sheet of wax paper. Put them in the refridgerator until set.

FRUITS

My name is BLUEBERRY...
I hold the magical energy of SELF ESTEEM,
TRUTH, COMPASSION and AUTHENTICITY...
I have a firm, silvery blue texture and a
mild, sweet flavor.
My gift to you is VALIDATION...
Imagine that my energy surrounds you
and TRUST that you are SAFE and that
you are LOVED.

FRUITS

BLUEBERRY PIE

2 deep dish frozen pie shells
2 cups BLUEBERRIES
6 tbsp sugar
3 tbsp corn starch
grated zest & juice of 1/2 orange
1/2 tsp cinnamon
whipped cream

Preheat oven to 400. In a large bowl, mix blueberries, sugar, cornstarch, zest, juice and cinnamon. Spoon into pie shell. Top the pie with the other pie shell, crimping the edges down. Bake for 30-35 minutes or until golden brown. Serve with a spoonful of whipped cream.

BEFORE YOU BEGIN, REMEMBER TO EMPOWER YOUR FRUIT (see page 4)

BLUEBERRY PANCAKES
Makes 10-12

1 cup of pancake mix	3/4 cup of milk
1 egg	1 tbsp oil

1/2 cup BLUEBERRIES,
fresh or frozen (thawed and drained)

Heat a skillet over med/low. Combine all the ingredients, except for the blueberries. Mix the batter until smooth. Then stir in the blueberries. Pour 1/4 cup batter for each pancake onto a lightly greased skillet. Turn when bottoms are golden brown. Serve with your favorite syrup.

My name is PEAR...
I hold the magical energy of
GRATIFICATION, LOVE, INTEGRITY and
PLEASURE...
My creamy white flesh is juicy and sweet.
My gift to you is ENJOYMENT...
Imagine that my energy surrounds you and
TRUST that you are SAFE and that
you are LOVED.

FRUITS

PEAR AND NUT SALAD
Serves 6-8

8 cups of lettuce, chopped
1 cup toasted nuts, chopped
3 PEARS, sliced thin
2 tbsp lemon juice
1 cup fresh strawberries, cut up

VINAIGRETTE
Makes 1 cup
1/3 cup balsamic vinegar
1 tsp garlic powder
2/3 cup extra virgin olive oil
Salt and pepper to taste

BEFORE YOU BEGIN, REMEMBER TO EMPOWER YOUR FRUIT (see page 4)

For the dressing, mix together the vinegar, garlic, salt and pepper. Add the oil and whisk until blended. In a small bowl, add the pears and lemon juice. Stir well to keep from discoloring. In a large bowl, add the lettuce nuts, pears, and berries.
Toss with vinaigrette and serve.

My name is APPLE...
I hold the magical energy of LOVE,
INSPIRATION, COMMITMENT and RENEWAL...
I am the most popular of all the fruits. My
crisp texture ranges from sweet to sour.
My gift to you is CREATIVITY...
Imagine that my energy surrounds you and
TRUST that you are SAFE and that
you are LOVED.

FRUITS

APPLE PIE WITH WALNUT CRUMB TOPPING

3 Granny Smith APPLES, peeled & thinly sliced
1/2 cup sugar
2 tbsp flour
1 tbsp lemon juice
1/2 tsp cinnamon
1 deep dish frozen pie shell
TOPPING:
1/2 cup flour
1/2 cup light brown sugar
1/2 cup walnuts, chopped
1/2 tsp cinnamon
1/4 tsp ground nutmeg
6 tbsp cold unsalted butter (cut into sections)

Preheat oven to 400. For the filling: In a large bowl, add the apples, sugar, flour, lemon juice, and cinnamon. Mix well and spoon into the pie shell. In a bowl, mix together all the ingredients for the topping until it forms crumbs. Sprinkle on top of the pie. Bake for 30-40 minutes or until golden brown. Let cool before serving.

BEFORE YOU BEGIN, REMEMBER TO EMPOWER YOUR FRUIT (see page 4)

APPLES WITH PORT WINE

4 martini glasses
4 small APPLES, (any kind you like)
cored & cut into chunks
2 tbsp lemon juice
1 bottle of port wine

In a small bowl, add the apples and lemon juice. Mix and let stand a few minutes. Pour out excess juice and add the wine (enough to coat). Let marinate for up to 1 hour. Spoon apples and wine evenly into glasses and top with whipped cream.

My name is CHERRY...
I hold the magical energy of LOVE,
SPIRITUAL WISDOM, TRANQUILITY
and TENDERNESS...
I have firm, deep red skin and a juicy,
sweet flavor.
My gift to you is INTIMACY...
Imagine that my energy surrounds you and
TRUST that you are SAFE and that
you are LOVED.

FRUITS

CHOCOLATE CHERRY PUDDING

2 boxes of 4-serving each instant
chocolate pudding
1 cup fresh or frozen (thawed) CHERRIES, halved
12 chocolate covered graham
cracker cookies, chopped
4 dessert glasses
2-3 tbsp chocolate chips

Prepare pudding according to directions. Reserve half the cherries and pudding. Layer the cherries, pudding, and the cookies equally into each glass. Then add the remaining cherries and pudding. Top with chocolate chips.

BEFORE YOU BEGIN, REMEMBER TO EMPOWER YOUR FRUIT (see page 4)

CHERRY VANILLA ICE CREAM CUPS
Serves 4

1 quart vanilla ice cream
1 cup frozen or fresh CHERRIES, chopped
1 jar hot fudge, warmed
1/2 cup nuts, chopped
4 dessert glasses

Add one scoop of ice cream to each dessert glass. Layer with hot fudge, nuts, and cherries. Top with another scoop of ice cream and drizzle with hot fudge. Garnish with a cherry.

FRUITS

My name is ORANGE...
I hold the magical energy of LOVE,
PROSPERITY, RISK and SUCCESS...
I have thick, orange skin, a pleasing,
citrus scent, and a juicy sweet flavor.
My gift to you is FAITH...
Imagine that my energy surrounds you and
TRUST that you are SAFE and that
you are LOVED.

FRUITS

ORANGE CREAMSICLE
Serves 4

4 dessert glasses
1 pint vanilla ice cream
4 oz ORANGE liqueur
zest of 1 ORANGE
4 thin slices of ORANGE

Scoop ice cream into glasses. Top with 1 oz orange liqueur
per glass. Garnish with orange slices and zest.

BEFORE YOU BEGIN, REMEMBER TO EMPOWER YOUR FRUIT (see page 4)

CHOPPED SALAD WITH CREAMY ORANGE DRESSING

2 seedless ORANGES, thinly sliced
8 oz mixed lettuce, torn
2-3 tbsp toasted pecans
4 oz croutons
2 ripe avocados, cubed

DRESSING
1 tbsp grated ORANGE zest
2/3 cup ORANGE juice
1 tsp fresh ginger, grated
2 tbsp sugar
3/4 cup plain yogurt

Beat together all the dressing ingredients and chill. For 2-3
hours. In a large bowl, add the lettuce, oranges, pecans,
croutons and avocados. Pour dressing over salad, toss and
serve.

My name is PINEAPPLE...
I hold the magical energy of MODESTY,
WEALTH, HONOR and APPRECIATION...
I have a large, pine cone-like texture and
spiky, green leaves. I have a warm, fruity
aroma and a sweet, acidic taste.
My gift to you is ACKNOWLEDGMENT...
Imagine that my energy surrounds you and
TRUST that you are SAFE and that
you are LOVED.

FRUITS

BAKED HAM WITH PINEAPPLE ORZO

2-3 lb baked ham
8 oz fresh or canned PINEAPPLES, sliced
1/2 cup PINEAPPLE juice
handful of cloves
ORZO
1/2 lb orzo
8 slices bacon
1/4 cup PINEAPPLE juice
1 cup PINEAPPLE chunks
3 scallions, chopped
4 cups chicken stock

BEFORE YOU BEGIN, REMEMBER TO EMPOWER YOUR FRUIT (see page 4)

Place ham in a baking dish. Use the cloves to secure the pineapple slices to the ham; covering completely. Pour pineapple juice over the ham and bake according to weight. In a saucepan, add the chicken stock and bring to a boil. Add the orzo and cook until all the liquid is absorbed, stirring frequently. In a large frying pan, cook the bacon until crisp. Remove and set aside. Add the scallions and pineapple chunks and saute in bacon drippings for 3-4 minutes. Add the pineapple juice, stir and scrape up all the dripping from the bottom of the pan. Bring to a boil and reduce heat. Add the cooked orzo and the crumbled bacon. Mix well and serve with ham.

My name is PEACH...
I hold the magical energy of DESIRE,
LOVE, LOYALTY and SEXUALITY...
I am known as the queen of the fruits.
My velvety skin is smooth and
my taste, deliciously sweet.
My gift to you is INITIATIVE...
Imagine that my energy surrounds you and
TRUST that you are SAFE and that
you are LOVED.

FRUITS

PEACH DELIGHT

4 martini or dessert glasses, chilled
1 pint PEACH flavored ice cream or sherbet
4 PEACHES fresh or canned, sliced thin
16 vanilla wafers
PEACH flavored liqueur or fruit juice
whipped cream

Place 4 wafers around the inside of each glass. Add 1 scoop of ice cream in the middle; 3-4 slices of peaches around the rim. Drizzle with liqueur or juice and top with whipped cream.

BEFORE YOU BEGIN, REMEMBER TO EMPOWER YOUR FRUIT (see page 4)

PEACH MARGARITA
Serves 4

juice of 2 limes
1 tray ice cubes
4 shots tequila
2 shots PEACH liqueur
garnish with fresh or canned PEACHES

Add all the ingredients into a blender and mix until smooth. Spoon into glasses. Garnish with peaches and serve.

My name is RASPBERRY...
I hold the magical energy of ENJOYMENT,
LOVE, ATTRACTION and STRENGTH...
My deep red, jewel-like texture has a
wonderfully, sweet flavor.
My gift to you is OPTIMISM...
Imagine that my energy surrounds you and
TRUST that you are SAFE and that
you are LOVED.

FRUITS

CHOPPED SALAD WITH RASPBERRY DRESSING
Serves 4

8 cups mixed lettuce, torn
2 cups RASPBERRIES
1 cup cherry tomatoes
4 oz mozzarella cheese, cubed
3 celery sticks, chopped
1 cucumber, sliced thin
1 red onion, sliced thin

DRESSING
1/4 cup RASPBERRY vinegar
(If you can't find use balsamic)
2 tbsp extra virgin olive oil
1 tsp garlic powder
2 tsp honey
2 tsp Dijon mustard
salt and pepper to taste

BEFORE YOU BEGIN, REMEMBER TO EMPOWER YOUR FRUIT (see page 4)

In a small bowl, mix together all the ingredients for the dressing. Place lettuce in a large bowl. Add raspberries, tomatoes, cheese, onion, cucumber and celery. Pour dressing over salad, toss and serve.

My name is PLUM...
I hold the magical energy of LOVE,
INSPIRATION, COMMITMENT and BALANCE...
I have smooth skin and a juicy,
pleasing taste.
My gift to you is ENTHUSIASM...
Imagine that my energy surrounds you and
TRUST that you are SAFE and that
you are LOVED.

FRUITS

PORK AND PLUM STIR FRY
Serves 4

2 red bell peppers, sliced thin
1 tbsp extra virgin olive oil
1 lb pork tenderloin , cut into strips
1 tbsp cornstarch plus 1 1/2 tsp
2 carrots, shredded
3 scallions, chopped
2 cloves garlic, finely chopped
1 lb pitted PLUMS cut into wedges
1 cup chicken stock
2 tbsp PLUM jam
1 tbsp cider vinegar
1 tbsp soy sauce
salt and pepper to taste

BEFORE YOU BEGIN, REMEMBER TO EMPOWER YOUR FRUIT (see page 4)

In a large pan, add the oil, 1 tbsp cornstarch, and pork. Cook over high heat until done. Remove pork to a plate. Reduce heat to medium. Add carrots, scallions, peppers, garlic, salt and pepper and cook 4-5 minutes. Then add the plums and cook an additional 4-5 minutes until plums are soft. In a small bowl, mix together the stock, jam, vinegar, soy sauce and remaining cornstarch. Pour into skillet and bring to a boil. Reduce to a simmer. Add pork back into the pan and cook until heated through.

My name is PLANTAIN..
I hold the magical energy of SUPPORT,
INNER POWER, COURAGE and PATIENCE...
Although I resemble the banana, I am
flatter in shape and have a firm,
less sweet taste.
My gift to you is HARMONY...
Imagine that my energy surrounds you and
TRUST that you are SAFE and that
you are LOVED.

FRUITS

PLANTAIN SPINACH ROUNDS
Serves 4

2 large ripe PLANTAINS, cut into 8 long slices
Oil for frying
2 tbsp butter
2 tbsp onion, finely chopped
2 cloves garlic, chopped
1 lb fresh spinach, chopped
pinch of ground nutmeg
1 egg
flour for dusting
salt and pepper, to taste

BEFORE YOU BEGIN, REMEMBER TO EMPOWER YOUR FRUIT (see page 4)

In a large frying pan, heat the oil and fry the plantains on both sides until golden but not fully cooked. Drain on paper towel and Reserve the oil. Add the butter, onion and garlic, and cook until tender. Add the spinach and nutmeg. Cover and cook until spinach has reduced. Drain excess moisture. Curl plantains into a ring and secure with a toothpick. Pack the middle of each one with a little spinach mixture. Place the egg and flour in separate bowls. Add more oil to the pan if necessary. Dip plantains into the egg and flour and fry on both sides until golden brown. Drain on paper towel.
Serve hot or cold.

My name is LIME...
I hold the magical energy of LOVE,
SECURITY, WELL-BEING and ACCEPTANCE...
My green skin is highly fragrant and my
taste is sour and acidic.
My gift to you is SERENITY...
Imagine that my energy surrounds you and
TRUST that you are SAFE and that
you are LOVED.

FRUITS

LIME CHICKEN
Serves 4

8 boneless chicken breasts, thinly sliced
2 scallions, chopped
1 tsp dried thyme
2 garlic cloves, finely chopped
juice of 2 LIMES
2 tbsp extra virgin olive oil
1 tbsp cilantro, chopped
2 cups cooked rice
salt and pepper to taste

BEFORE YOU BEGIN, REMEMBER TO EMPOWER YOUR FRUIT (see page 4)

In a small bowl, add the scallions, thyme, garlic, lime juice, cilantro, salt and pepper, and mix well. Pour over chicken, coating well, and let marinate for a couple of hours. In a large frying pan, add the oil and chicken, and cook until no longer pink. Cut the limes into slices and garnish. Serve with your favorite rice.

My name is LEMON...
I hold the magical energy of LOVE,
COMPANIONSHIP, COMMITMENT
and AUTHENTICITY...
My skin contains aromatic, essential oils
and I have a refreshing, juicy, acidic taste.
My gift to you is ROMANCE...
Imagine that my energy surrounds you and
TRUST that you are SAFE and that
you are LOVED.

FRUITS

LEMON FLOUNDER
Serves 4

4 filets of flounder
1 cup flour (enough to coat)
2 tbsp extra virgin olive oil
1/4 cup LEMON juice
3 garlic cloves, finely chopped
2 tbsp butter
3 scallions, chopped
1/2 cup chicken stock
1 tsp sugar
2 tbsp parsley, chopped

BEFORE YOU BEGIN, REMEMBER TO EMPOWER YOUR FRUIT (see page 4)

Coat fish in the flour. In a large frying pan, add 1 tbsp oil and 1 tbsp butter. Add the fish and cook until golden brown on one side before flipping or it may break a part. Cook other side until golden and remove to a plate to keep warm. Add to the pan 1 tbsp oil and 1 tbsp butter. Add the scallions and garlic, cook a few minutes, then add the stock, parsley, sugar, lemon juice, salt and pepper. Scrape the bottom of the pan to get all the bits and pieces, and bring to a boil. Cook a few minutes. Pour sauce over fish and serve.

My name is GRAPE...
I hold the magical energy of WISDOM,
ABUNDANCE, SEDUCTION and CREATIVITY...
I grow in bunches on a stalk and my firm,
crisp pulp is succulent and sweet.
My gift to you is MAGNETISM...
Imagine that my energy surrounds you and
TRUST that you are SAFE and that
you are LOVED.

FRUITS

CHOPPED SALAD WITH FRESH GRAPES

8 cups torn lettuce greens
2 cups seedless GRAPES, halved
1 8-oz can of black olives, sliced
1 small red onion, sliced thin
1 cup walnuts, coarsely chopped
4 oz cheddar cheese, cubed
1 cucumber, sliced thin

RASPBERRY DRESSING
3 tbsp raspberry vinegar
1 small sweet onion, finely chopped
1 tsp garlic powder
1/2 cup extra virgin olive oil

BEFORE YOU BEGIN, REMEMBER TO EMPOWER YOUR FRUIT (see page 4)

In a large bowl, add lettuce, grapes, olives, onion, cucumber, walnuts and cheese. In a small bowl, add the vinegar (if you can't find raspberry, use balsamic) onion, garlic, oil, salt and pepper. Mix well and pour over salad. Toss and serve with your favorite crusty bread.

My name is BANANA...
I hold the magical energy of AFFLUENCE,
POWER, GROWTH and CHOICE...
I have an easy to peel, yellow skin and
sweet, creamy white flesh.
My gift to you is INSPIRATION...
Imagine that my energy surrounds you and
TRUST that you are SAFE and that
you are LOVED.

FRUITS

BANANA CREAM PIE

1 ready made graham cracker crust pie shell
3 packages 4 servings each
instant vanilla pudding
4 large BANANAS, sliced thin
12 oz ready made whipped cream

In a large bowl, prepare pudding according to directions.
Add 6 oz whipped cream and banana slices. Mix together
and spoon into pie shell. Top with remaining whipped cream
and chill for 1 hour.

BEFORE YOU BEGIN, REMEMBER TO EMPOWER YOUR FRUIT (see page 4)

CHOCOLATE DIPPED BANANAS

4 large BANANAS
4 pop sickle sticks
14 oz quality chocolate
TOPPINGS
nuts, coconut or chocolate chips

Bring approximately 2 inches of water to a boil. Place a
metal bowl over top of boiling pot, add chocolate, and melt.
Line a cookie tin with wax paper. Push pop sickle sticks into
the bottom of each banana until secure. Dip bananas in
melted chocolate and roll in your favorite topping. Chill in
refrigerator until set.

FRUITS

My name is TOMATO...
I hold the magical energy of SUCCESS,
RESPONSIBILITY, SELF LOVE, and
FULFILLMENT...
I come in all shapes and sizes and have a
juicy, delightful flavor.
My gift to you is SIGNIFICANCE...
Imagine that my energy surrounds you and
TRUST that you are SAFE and that
you are LOVED.

FRUITS

BRUSCHETTA
Makes about 30

1 large loaf French or Italian bread sliced 1/2 thick
4 plum TOMATOES seeded and chopped
1/2 cup fresh basil
3 tbsp extra virgin olive oil
1 tsp garlic powder
1 small sweet onion, finely chopped
salt and pepper to taste

In a large bowl, add the tomatoes, onion, basil, garlic, salt, pepper and 2 tbsp oil, and mix well. Brush sliced bread with remaining oil on both sides and toast until golden brown. Spread tomato mixture on top of bread and serve.

BEFORE YOU BEGIN, REMEMBER TO EMPOWER YOUR FRUIT (see page 4)

FLOUNDER PARMIGIANA
Serves 4

8 oz shredded mozzarella cheese
4 cloves garlic, chopped
2 cups flavored bread crumbs
1 small onion, chopped
28 oz can crushed TOMATOES

1 egg
4 filets of flounder
4 oz basil, chopped
salt and pepper to taste
1/4 cup olive oil

In a large saucepan, add 2 tbsp oil, 2 garlic cloves, onion, and saute until tender. Add the tomatoes, salt, pepper and 2 oz basil. Stir and cook on med/low for about 30 minutes. In a large frying pan, add remaining oil. Beat the egg in a small bowl. Mix together the bread crumbs, 2 cloves garlic and remaining basil. Dip the flounder in the egg and coat with bread crumbs. Cook until golden brown on one side, then flip over, and cook until golden..Transfer to a baking dish, cover with tomato sauce, and top with cheese . Broil until cheese is melted.

FRUITS

My name is NUT...
I hold the magical energy of FREEDOM,
VULNERABILITY, RESPONSIBILITY
and COURAGE...
I am a one-celled fruit encased in a
dry shell.
I have a fragrant scent and robust flavor.
My gift to you is SPONTANEITY...
Imagine that my energy surrounds you and
TRUST that you are SAFE and that
you are LOVED.

FRUITS

PEANUT BUTTER CHOCOLATE CHIP COOKIES
Makes about 3 dozen

1 cup crunchy PEANUT butter	3 tbsp milk
1/2 cup butter, softened	1 tbsp vanilla
1 1/4 cups light brown sugar	1 egg
1 3/4 cups flour	3/4 tsp salt
3/4 tsp baking soda	12 oz bag chocolate chips

Preheat oven to 375. In a large bowl, combine peanut butter, brown sugar, milk, vanilla, flour, salt, baking soda and egg. Mix together well. Add the chocolate chips and mix again. Drop heaping teaspoonfuls onto baking sheet and bake for 8-10 minutes or until lightly browned. Cool and serve.

BEFORE YOU BEGIN, REMEMBER TO EMPOWER YOUR FRUIT (see page 4)

CHOCOLATE COATED NUT CLUSTERS
Makes about 20-24 pieces

1 cup each almond & pecan NUTS
12 oz chocolate, chopped into small pieces
wax paper

Preheat oven to 375. Roast nuts in the oven until toasted. Remove and cool. Melt the chocolate in a heat proof bowl over a pan of barely simmering water. Remove from the heat, but leave the bowl over the water so that the chocolate remains liquid. Place the wax paper over a baking sheet. Add the nuts to the chocolate and stir to coat. Using two spoons, scoop up a cluster of nuts and place them on the baking sheet.
Refrigerate until set.

FRUITS

My name is COCONUT...
I hold the magical energy of SIMPLICITY,
FREEDOM, BALANCE and PEACE...
My juicy nectar is sweet and my
taste, delicious.
My gift to you is JOY...
Imagine that my energy surrounds you and
TRUST that you are SAFE and that
you are LOVED.

FRUITS

COCONUT CHOCOLATE CHIP ANGEL FOOD CAKE

1 bundt pan
1 box angel food cake mix
12 oz package semi-sweet chocolate chips
2 cups toasted COCONUT
chocolate sauce (any kind you like)

Preheat oven to 375. Prepare cake mix according to directions. Add the chocolate chips and 1 1/2 cups of coconut to the batter. Mix well and pour into the pan. Bake for 35-45 minutes. When the cake is done, let cool, then drizzle the chocolate sauce over the top.
Sprinkle with remaining coconut and serve.

BEFORE YOU BEGIN, REMEMBER TO EMPOWER YOUR FRUIT (see page 4)

COCONUT CREAM PIE

1 ready made graham cracker pie shell
3 boxes of 4 serving instant vanilla pudding
12 oz ready made whipped cream
2 cups toasted COCONUT
1 cup almonds, chopped

In a large bowl, prepare the pudding according to directions, then combine with 6 oz whipped cream and coconut. Mix well and spoon into the shell. Spread remaining whipped cream over the top and sprinkle with chopped almonds. Serve immediately or refrigerate.

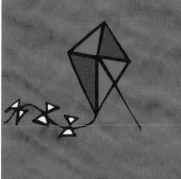

KID FRIENDLY
RECIPES

MACARONI AND CHEESE
Serves 4-6

1 lb elbow macaroni
1 lb American cheese, sliced
(save some for the topping)
28 oz can crushed TOMATOES
SALT and PEPPER to taste
6 fresh BASIL leaves, chopped

Preheat oven to 350. In a bowl, add the tomato sauce, basil, salt and pepper, and mix well. Cook pasta according to directions. In a baking dish, layer the bottom with the sauce, macaroni, then cheese; keep layering until dish is filled. Top with remaining cheese and bake for 30-35 minutes.

SPINACH SOUP
Serves 8

1/2 cup ONION, chopped
1 GARLIC clove, chopped
2 tbsp butter
3 CARROT sticks, diced
3 CELERY sticks, diced
6 cups chicken stock
1/2 cup uncooked acinipepe pasta
1/4 tsp ground NUTMEG
SALT and PEPPER to taste
10 oz fresh SPINACH (can use frozen)
Parmesan cheese (optional)

In a large saucepan, add the butter, onion and garlic and saute until tender. Add the carrots and celery and saute for about 8 minutes. Add the chicken stock and bring to a boil. Add the pasta, nutmeg, salt and pepper, and simmer for about 5-7 minutes. Add the fresh spinach and cook for about 5 minutes. Top with cheese and serve.

CINNAMON TOAST
Serves 4

4 slices of bread (any kind you like)
butter (enough to spread)
1 tbsp SUGAR
1 tsp CINNAMON

Lightly toast the bread. In a small bowl, mix together the sugar and cinnamon. Spread the butter over all 4 slices. Sprinkle with sugar mixture and serve.

SUGARED BANANAS

4 BANANAS peeled & sliced
2 tbsp SUGAR
whipped cream

Mix sugar and bananas together and spoon into a cup. Top with whipped cream and serve.

PASTA WITH MEAT SAUCE
Serves 4

1 lb chopped beef or turkey breast
28 oz can crushed TOMATOES
1/2 small ONION, chopped
3 GARLIC cloves, chopped
6 fresh BASIL leaves, chopped
SALT and PEPPER to taste
2 tbsp extra virgin olive oil
1 lb pasta (any kind you like)

In a large frying pan, cook the meat until no longer pink. Remove and place on the side. Add to the pan the oil, onion and garlic, and saute until tender. Add back the meat and cook 2 minutes. Add the tomato sauce, basil, salt and pepper. Cook on med/low heat for 30 minutes. Cook pasta according to directions, drain and toss with meat sauce. Serve with Parmesan cheese.

MEATBALL SOUP

1 lb chopped turkey breast or beef
3 CARROTS, finely chopped
3 CELERY sticks, finely chopped
2 BAY leaves
1 medium ONION, chopped
SALT and PEPPER to taste
1 egg
2 cloves GARLIC, finely chopped
1/2 cup flavored bread crumbs
1/2 cup PARSLEY, finely chopped
1/2 cup parmesan cheese (optional)
6 cups chicken stock
2 cups water
1 1/2 cups orzo or ditalini
1 lb fresh SPINACH, chopped

In a large saucepan, add the stock, water, onion, carrots, celery, bay leaves, salt and pepper and let cook until the vegetables are tender. In a bowl, combine the bread crumbs, chopped meat, egg, garlic, cheese, parsley, salt and pepper. Form into very small meatballs. When soup is ready, bring up to a boil and drop in meatballs. Let cook a few minutes, then add the pasta and stir. Cover and simmer for 10 minutes or until pasta is tender. When pasta is done, add the chopped spinach until wilted. Remove from heat and serve.

ICE CREAM PIE

1 cup shredded COCONUT
3 oz chopped NUTS
1 1/2 cups CHOCOLATE chips
1 quart VANILLA ice cream
1 ready made graham cracker pie shell
6 oz ready made whipped cream
hot fudge

Leave ice cream to soften. In a small bowl, mix together 2 oz nuts, 1 cup chocolate chips, and 3/4 cup coconut. Add the softened ice cream and mix well. Warm the hot fudge and spread enough into pie shell, coating the bottom and sides well. Spoon in the ice cream mixture and spread evenly. Top with whipped cream and sprinkle with remaining coconut, chips and nuts. Chill for 1 hour. Right before serving, drizzle hot fudge across the top.

KID FRIENDLY RECIPES

MARINARA SAUCE
(To be used for pizza & fried sticks)

28 oz can crushed TOMATOES
3 GARLIC cloves, chopped
5-6 fresh BASIL leaves
1 small ONION, chopped
SALT and PEPPER to taste

In large saucepan, add the oil, onion and garlic, and saute until tender. Add the tomato sauce, basil, salt and pepper. Stir to combine. Cook on low for 30 minutes.

FRIED MOZZARELLA STICKS

1 lb frozen mozzarella, sliced into sticks
(freeze mozzarella ahead of time)
2 eggs
1 cup flavored bread crumbs
3 GARLIC cloves, finely chopped
1 handful of fresh PARSLEY, finely chopped
SALT and PEPPER to taste
oil for frying
marinara dipping sauce

Mix the eggs in a small bowl and set a side. Mix together the bread crumbs, garlic, parsley, salt and pepper. In a large pan, heat up 1/4 inch oil. Dip the frozen cheese into the egg and coat with the bread crumb mixture. Fry until golden brown. To keep it lean, try baking them. Heat the oven to 450. Lightly coat the top of each one with some oil and bake until golden. Serve with above marinara sauce.

KID FRIENDLY RECIPES

ENGLISH MUFFIN PIZZAS
Serves 4-6

4 sandwich sized English muffins, cut in half
marinara sauce
8 oz mozzarella cheese, shredded

On a baking pan, add the muffins and spread the marinara sauce over each section, covering thoroughly. Sprinkle a handful of cheese on top and broil until muffins are toasted and cheese is melted. Add some of your favorite toppings.

ITALIAN PASTA SALAD

1 lb tricolor rottini pasta
2 green peppers, finely chopped
8 oz black olives, chopped
1 cup Italian dressing

ITALIAN DRESSING
2 tbsp red wine vinegar
1 tsp Dijon MUSTARD
2 tsp water
2 tsp GARLIC powder
SALT and PEPPER to taste
1/2 cup extra virgin olive oil

This is my niece, Amanda's favorite dish (she's 7). Cook pasta according to directions and place in the refrigerator to cool. In a small bowl, whisk together all the ingredients for the dressing, except the oil. Then in a steady stream, slowly whisk in the oil. Once pasta is cooled, add the peppers, olives and dressing.
Mix together and chill for 1 hour.

MINI BURGER BITS
Makes about 10-12

1 1/4 lb ground sirloin
4 cloves GARLIC, finely chopped
3 SCALLIONS finely chopped (including greens)
1 tbsp PAPRIKA
6 oz can TOMATO paste
1/2 cup CILANTRO or PARSLEY, finely chopped
SALT and PEPPER
ready to bake biscuits
8 z shredded cheese, (any kind you like)

Mix together the sirloin, garlic, scallions, paprika, tomato paste, cilantro (for milder taste use parsley), salt and pepper. Form into meatball size and flatten like a burger. You should get between 10-12 mini burgers. Bake biscuits according to directions. Grill or broil burgers until desired taste. The last minute of grilling, top with shredded cheese.
　　Use biscuits as your bun and serve.

LEMONADE

1 1/2 cups SUGAR or to taste
12 LEMON zest strips
1 1/2 cups LEMON juice
water

Add the sugar, lemon zest, and lemon juice
into a pitcher. Fill the rest of the pitcher with
water to the rim. Stir and let chill.
Fill glasses with ice and pour.

HOT CHOCOLATE

4 cups milk
1 tsp CINNAMON
2 whole CLOVES
4 oz milk CHOCOLATE, chopped into pieces
1/4 tsp VANILLA

In a medium saucepan, heat the milk,
cinnamon, cloves, and vanilla until boiling.
Stir in the chocolate until melted. Pour into
a blender and mix on high speed until frothy
(about 30 seconds). Pour into cups and top
with whipped cream .

INDEX

INDEX